ALEXANDRIA LOST

*From the Advent of Christianity to
the Arab Conquest*

Bojana Mojsov

Duckworth

First published in 2010 by
Gerald Duckworth & Co. Ltd.
90-93 Cowcross Street, London EC1M 6BF
Tel: 020 7490 7300
Fax: 020 7490 0080
info@duckworth-publishers.co.uk
www.ducknet.co.uk

A catalogue record for this book is available
from the British Library

ISBN 978 0 7156 3865 1

Typeset by Ray Davies
Printed and bound in Great Britain by
CPI Antony Rowe, Chippenham and Eastbourne

Contents

Preface and Acknowledgements

What happened to ancient Alexandria and to the Great Library? Alexander's city was the shining star of the Mediterranean Sea, the museum the pride of the classical world, the library the greatest collection of antiquity. How could they disappear so thoroughly, without a trace? This book attempts to find some of the answers by taking a closer look at events that took place between the advent of Christianity in 391 and the Arab conquest in 646. Much of the information in it comes from people who have devoted their lives' work to recovering and preserving the city's historical heritage, among them Jean-Yves Empereur, Mustafa el Abbadi, Mohammed Awad and Mona Hagag. Many friends have graciously extended their help, encouragement and assistance: Norma-Jean Bothmer, Roland and Susan Chambers, Matthew Connolly, Nenad Mikalacki-Django, Lili Doss, Richard Hoare, Hisham Mehrez, Svetlana and Michel Nussenzweig, Alan Rush, Matthew Sturgis, Patrick Werr and Olga Vassilieva. Julian Reilly was a source of constant strength and support and took the photographs for the book. I would like to thank them all.

I would also like to thank the National Museum in Alexandria and the Pushkin Museum of Fine Arts in Moscow for granting permission to publish several objects in their collections for the first time.

A note about the illustrations: how does one illustrate the tale of a vanished city? Not one of the historical monuments of Alexandria has survived. Archaeological finds are few and fortuitous; we have no material traces of the events described in this book nor any portraits of the main protagonists. The chance objects that have come down to us through the ages throw but a faint, oblique light on this obscure period of history and illustrate the story tangentially, by association. Nevertheless, I hope that they can help restore a part of the missing record and give some idea about the art of the time. Finally, the title: it refers to the ancient city that lies buried under the new. Modern Alexandria is a lively, thriving metropolis building its way into the future.

Illustrations

Illustrations

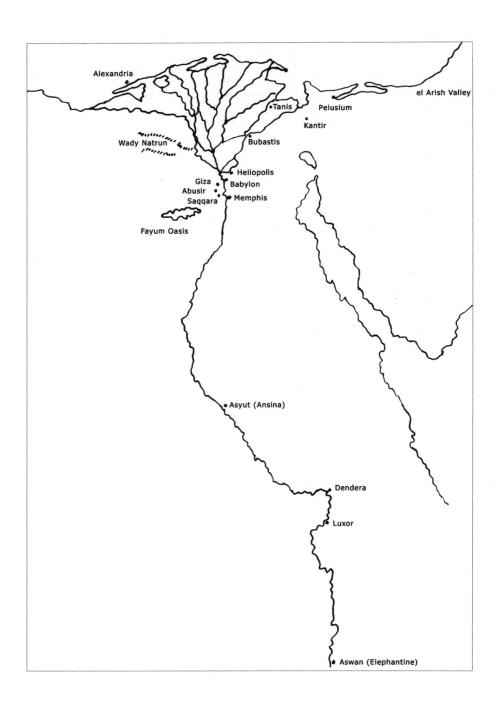

Alexandria

el Arish Valley

•Tanis

Pelusium

Kantir

Wady Natrun

Bubastis

Heliopolis

Giza
Abusir
Saqqara

Babylon

Memphis

Fayum Oasis

• Asyut (Ansina)

Dendera

• Luxor

• Aswan (Elephantine)

10

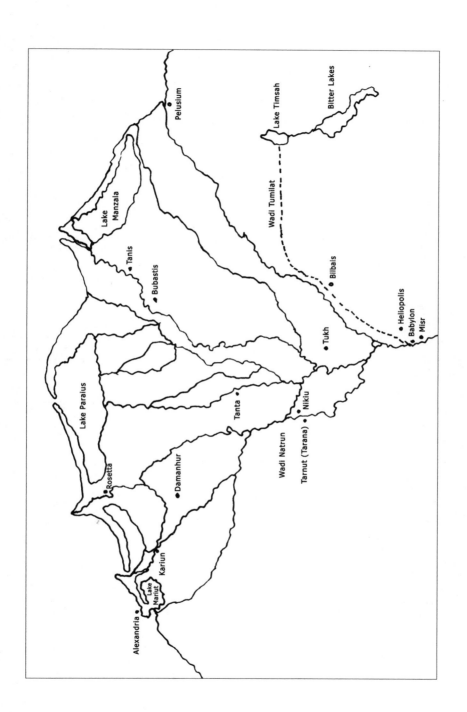

Alexander's City

Alexandria. At last, Alexandria. Lady of the Dew. Bloom of white nimbus. Bosom of radiance, wet with sky water. Core of nostalgia steeped in honey and tears.

Naguib Mahfouz, *Miramar* (1967)

The story of Alexandria begins with Alexander the Great. Having conquered Egypt, Alexander went riding west along Egypt's Mediterranean coast, looking for a place to establish a seaport with a large Greek colony. He was about to mark a site on the advice of his architects, when during the night he had a dream. In his dream, he saw a hoary old man with a venerable air standing on an empty beach. The man smiled at him and recited three verses from the *Odyssey*:

There lies an island in the churning sea
Hard against the Egyptian shore,
Pharos is the name men give it.

The next morning Alexander set out to find Pharos. Riding along the shore, he came across a small island lying opposite a limestone ridge that jutted out of a harbour resembling a wide isthmus. The ridge ran the whole length between the sea and a vast lagoon with a freshwater lake. Alexander said that Homer, among so many other admirable talents, also possessed that of an architect, and he ordered his soldiers to mark the area. No chalk could be found to hand, so the soldiers used barley to draw the circumference. The overall plan of the walls drawn by the barley seeds suggested the shape of a *chlamys*, a short Greek cloak, tapering evenly from the bottom edge. They were standing, contemplating the plan, when a flock of birds flew from the shore and ate some of the barley. Alexander asked his soothsayers if this was a good omen. Take heart, they said, the omen means the city will prosper and have enough food to feed many mouths.[1]

The task of building Alexandria fell to Ptolemy Lagos, Alexander's general, who came to rule Egypt after Alexander's death. The construction was continued by Ptolemy II Philadelphos and Ptolemy III Eugertes; by the end of the reign of Ptolemy III most of the buildings in the inner city had been completed. The streets were based on Aristotle's ideal urban plan; they were designed on a rectangular grid and oriented south-west to

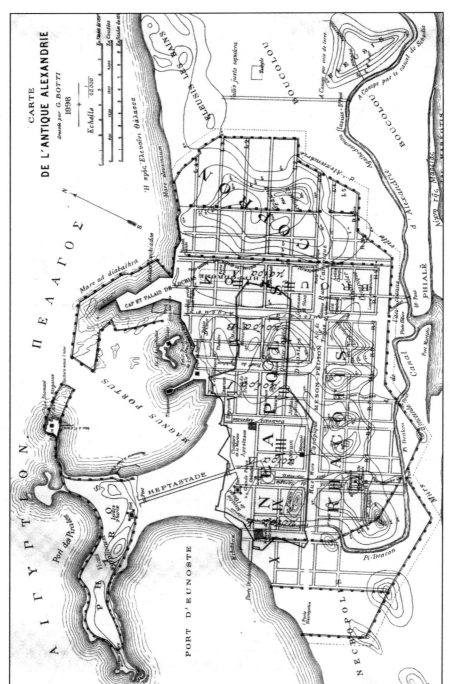

1. Map of ancient Alexandria drawn by G. Botti, Director of the Greco-Roman Museum, in 1898.

2. Reconstruction of the Pharos Lighthouse, after E. Tiersch.

provide shelter from the north wind and take advantage of the westerly
sea breeze.

The inner city was walled; there were four gates, the Canopic and the
Western on the east and west; the Gate of the Sun and the Gate of the Moon
on the north and south (fig. 1). A wide street between the Gates of the Sun
and Moon connected the lake harbour with the seashore. Between the
Canopic Gate and the Western Gate stretched the main street, the Canopic
Way, 3 miles long and 100 feet wide, paved with white marble and shaded
by colonnades. It was as bright by night as it was by day. A visitor to the
city described how awnings of green silk were hung over the walls to
relieve the dazzling brilliance of the marble. 'No one entered the city
without a covering over his eyes to veil him from the glare … By night the
moonlight reflected from the white marble made the city so bright, that a
tailor could see to thread his needle without a lamp.'[2]

Alexandria's lighthouse, built on the island of Pharos, was renowned as

15

one of the Seven Wonders of the World (fig. 2). It was completed in 280 BC and rose to a height of 311 feet. It was the first of a chain of beacons that stretched from Alexandria along the North African coast to Cyrene. The Pharos had three levels: a square cross-section, an octagonal tower and a cylindrical room at the top. The room sheltered a lantern that, according to Flavius Josephus, could be seen 300 stadia (30 miles) away. To throw a light that far a projector would have been necessary. We have no contemporary description or model of Alexandria's lantern, but the physicist Lucio Russo suggests that it was a parabolic mirror made according to the theory of the reversibility of optical paths. Such a theory appeared in Alexandria at precisely the time of the construction of the Pharos.[3] The lighthouse was dedicated to Isis Pharia, the protector of seafarers, and to the Dioscuri, Castor and Pollux.

From the sea shore a dyke 550 feet long, the *heptastadion*, connected the shore to the island of Pharos. This man-made bridge divided the coastline in two and broke the sea current. The city had two harbours, the Royal and *Eunostos*, the Port of Happy Returns. Behind the city the freshwater lake of Mariut, connected to the Nile by a canal, ensured a constant supply of water for the great cisterns built under the pavements.

The greatest temple in the city was dedicated to Serapis (fig. 3). It was built on Serapeum Hill, one of the city's few natural outcrops, grandly called the Acropolis, despite its modest proportions. The hill was artificially enlarged to include many vaulted sub-structures, storey upon storey, and from the outside it looked like a rectangular fortress. There were two ways of access to it: one by carriage road at the back (still visible today) and another by a long flight of steps on the eastern side.[4] At the top of the stairs a visitor entered the *propylaeum*, upheld by four columns, two on each side of the passage. It could be closed off by bronze gates.[5] Adjoining the *propylaeum* was an open shrine with a golden dome that rested on a double ring of columns.[6] The temple of Serapis was rectangular and housed a cult statue of Serapis made by the sculptor Bryaxis. Next to the Serapeum stood the Daughter Library. It was open to the public and according to the poet Callimachus contained 42,800 books. The temple contained a Nilometer that measured the annual floods of the Nile, and subterranean chambers used in the cult of the bull god.

At the heart of the classical city lay the Museion, the first public research institution,[7] and the Great Library, said to contain 700,000 scrolls. Ptolemy Lagos had purchased Aristotle's library and brought it from Athens to Alexandria to establish the core of the collection. The Museum and the Library were not open to the public but reserved for scholars who undertook research in philology, the mathematical sciences and astrology. Both institutions were famed for their accomplishments. The school of mathematics had been founded by Euclid in the fourth century BC and remained active until the time of Hypatia some 800 years later.

3. Cult statue of Serapis, third century BC, marble. National Museum,

The first director of the library, Eratosthenes, was the first person to calculate the circumference of the earth, coming within two per cent of modern measurements. In the third century BC Aristarchus of Samos determined the distance between the sun and the moon and realized that they existed within a heliocentric system. In medicine, Heraphilus had succeeded in isolating the arterial and nervous systems. The Museion had attracted such famous names as Archimedes of Syracuse who established some of the laws of physics and invented the Archimedes screw for raising Nile water, still used to irrigate the fields in the Delta. In the first century AD the mathematician Heron (also known as Hero of Alexandria) published the scientific classics *Pneumatica, Metrica* and *Mechanica*. The Ptolemaic kings also continued Aristotle's classification of the world's flora and fauna, a project begun in Athens by Aristotle and Theophrastus in the fourth century BC. They set up zoological and botanical gardens, where plant species from other parts of the world were acclimatized and grown commercially. In many ways this was where science as we know it was born.

In Roman times Alexandria became one the main ports of the Roman Empire. The geographer Strabo, who visited the city in the first century AD, described 120 ships setting sail to India, taking advantage of the monsoon winds on both legs of the voyage which lasted several months. A cargo of a single ship, *Horapollo*, returning from the port of Muziris on the western Indian coast, contained 60 cases of the aromatic plant spikenard, 5 tons of spices, more than 100 tons of elephant tusk, and 135 tons of ebony.[8] Strabo called Alexandria 'the Emporium of the World'. Greeks, Jews, Romans, Phoenicians, Nabataeans, Arabs and Indians traded on its markets. The teeming mass of people on the streets was described by Achilles Tatius: 'When I contemplated the city, I thought there could never be enough inhabitants to fill it entirely; but when I looked at the inhabitants I asked myself in amazement if there could ever be a city capable of containing them.'

Strabo described the inner city as occupying a very large area:

Everywhere the city is crisscrossed with roads capable of being used by horsemen or drivers of carts. Two of these streets are very broad, more than a *plethon* in width, and intersect at right angles. The city contains some splendid works and royal buildings, which occupy a quarter if not a third of the total area, for each of the kings, desirous in their turn to embellish the public buildings with some new ornaments, was no less desirous at adding at his own expense another residence to those already in existence.

The *Museion* too forms part of the royal buildings and comprises a *peripatos*, an *exedra* with seats. A large building houses the common room, where the scholars who are members of the *Museion* take their meals. The community of learned men enjoy common ownership of property and there is a priest who is the head of the *Museion*, in Greek times appointed by the kings, in Roman times by Caesar. The place called *Soma* also forms part of the royal buildings. The precinct houses the royal sepulchres and that of Alexander ...

As you enter the harbours, to your right you discover the island and tower of Pharos. To your left are the rocks of Cape Lochias, which has its own royal buildings. As you go further into the port, you will see on your left the royal building of the interior, which extends continuously from the Cape of Lochias, comprising wooded groves and numerous residences in a variety of styles. Below these buildings lies the man-made harbour, which is closed off, having formerly been the private property of the kings, now of Caesar. So too is Antirhodos, the island across the man made harbour, which has a royal palace and a little port of its own. It was so named because it was a rival of Rhodes itself.

Above the man-made harbour are the theatre and the Poseidion, a temple of Poseidon. Anthony extended the projection into the harbour at this point, by building a mall. At the end of the mall he built a royal residence by the name Timonium. Then come the Caesareum and the warehouses. After them the arsenals, which extend all the way to the *heptastadion*.

The city was well known for its arts and crafts. It had numerous workshops for sculpture, relief, painting and mosaic (figs 4, 5). Papyrus, textiles and glasswork were also traded. The main industry was shipbuilding; the Alexandrians were famous for building the largest galleys in the Mediterranean, the so-called *triremes* that could be used at war.

During the 800 years of its existence the classical city had been battered on many occasions. The Alexandrian mob was notorious for its ill temper, and frequent riots often damaged the city centre. The first serious loss was caused by the soldiers of Julius Caesar when they set fire to a building that stored some books from the Great Library during the Civil Wars of 43 BC. Later in 215 Caracalla wreaked havoc on the market, a densely populated area in the centre of the city, because the mob had risen in protest against his savage treatment of the Alexandrians. In 273 Aurelian destroyed the *Brucheion*, the Royal Quarter, when the supporters of Firmus, who had risen against Aurelian after his defeat of Palmyra, barricaded themselves within the walls. In the fourth century, Diocletian, while suppressing a revolt that was blamed on the Christians, damaged the area at the foot of the Serapeum.

After the advent of Christianity a different kind of destruction began. In 391-2 the Byzantine emperor Theodosius issued a decree that outlawed all forms of pagan worship in the Byzantine Empire. In the aftermath of the decree's enforcement, a mob led by Christian fanatics killed Hypatia, the last director of the Museion. Her public murder sparked the drawn-out but violent destruction of the entire legacy of the classical city, carried out with a thoroughness seldom rivalled in Christian history.

Two centuries of suppression of the pagans were followed by half a century of undeclared war between the Melkite Church of Constantinople and the Coptic Church of Egypt. It culminated in the violent persecution of the Copts by the Melkite patriarch Cyrus. In 639 the Arab armies began

4. Dog guarding a house, second-century AD mosaic from a Roman villa found in 1993 during the building of the new library. Archaeological Museum, *Biblioteca Alexandrina*, Alexandria.

5. Head of Medusa, second-century AD mosaic from a Roman villa. National Museum, Alexandria.

their advance on Egypt. Having spent ten years in hiding, the Copts of Egypt saw no alternative but to turn to them for help. They joined the Arabs in their fight against the Byzantines and within a year of the Arab invasion the Byzantines signed a treaty of surrender with the Arabs. On that occasion the great gates of Alexandria were flung open to welcome the Arab army and the Arab cavalry rode in triumph down the Canopic Way. The last Byzantine garrisons left Egypt in 642 after an eleven-month armistice.

Three years later the Alexandrians rose in revolt. They had lost their sea trade and could no longer pay the rising taxes imposed on non-Muslims. They invited the Byzantines to recapture the city, and in 645 a great Byzantine fleet of 300 ships sailed into the Royal Harbour without warning and anchored without resistance. Some 1,000 Arab soldiers left to defend the city were quickly overpowered and Alexandria was delivered once more into Byzantine hands. For almost a year the Byzantines held the city unchallenged. However, in the summer of 646 the Arabs returned, won the battle of Nikiu and pursued the scattered Byzantine army all the way to the walls of Alexandria. Then they took the city by force, set it on fire and demolished the surrounding walls.

Christianity in Egypt

According to the tradition of the Egyptian Coptic Church, Christianity was introduced to Alexandria by St Mark, who was martyred in AD 62 for protesting against the worship of Serapis. The earliest Christian centres were the Oratory of St Mark, which stood by the sea-shore,[1] and a church dedicated to the Virgin Mary.[2] Coptic tradition holds that St Mark heads the list of the patriarchs of Alexandria and that today's spiritual leader of the Coptic community, Pope Shenouda III, is his 117th successor (fig. 6).

The word *Copt* derives from the Greek *Aegyptos* via medieval *Kyptaios* and the Arabic *Qibt*. *Aegyptos* in turn derives from *Hikaptah*, 'House of the spirit (*ka*) of Ptah', which was one of the names of Memphis, the ancient capital of Egypt. The Arabs called Egypt *dar el Qibti*, 'home of the Egyptians', and as Christianity was then the official religion of Egypt, the Arabic word *Qibt* came to describe Christians as well as all the inhabitants of the Nile Valley. This was how the word *Copt* came to encapsulate the entire history of the people of Egypt.

At first, Christianity in Egypt was Judaeo-Christian in nature and the oldest Christian centres were inside Jewish ghettos. But deeper and more obscure than history, in the hearts of the Coptic faithful, lies the belief that the Holy Family escaped to Egypt and spent three years travelling through the country. One of their dwellings is believed to be a crypt under the sixth-century Church of St Sergius, near the Ben Ezra Synagogue in the Fort of Babylon (Old Cairo). The Hanging Church, regarded as the oldest surviving congregational church, was built nearby, on top of the Gate of Diocletian (figs 8, 9, 10, 11).

The Roman fort of Babylon was built by Trajan in AD 100; additions were made during the reign of Diocletian (284-305). According to John of Nikiu, the Roman building stood on top of an earlier fortress that was built by Nebuchadnezzar at the time of his invasion of Egypt in 664 BC, and this was how it came to have the same name as the capital of Babylonia. Josephus wrote that it had been built by the Persians under Cambyses (525-522 BC), while Eutychius named Artaxerxes Oxus (465-424 BC) as the original builder. Strabo, who visited Egypt 130 years before Trajan, described seeing a fort by the name of Babylon 'standing on a rocky ridge' on the Nile. He traced the name to some Babylonian exiles who had settled there at an unspecified time.

Archaeological evidence suggests a long occupation of the site. The Roman foundations stand on top of ancient Egyptian masonry; under the

6. The lion of St Mark, Coptic textile, sixth century. The Pushkin Museum of Fine Arts, Moscow.

7. St George, the four beasts of the apocalypse and the lion of St Mark, Coptic textile, sixth century. The Pushkin Museum of Fine Arts, Moscow.

8. The Gate of Diocletian with the Hanging Church above. The Fort of Babylon (old Cairo).

9. Restored ramparts of the Fort of Babylon.

10. The walls of the Fort of Babylon and the gate of the Hanging Church.

11. Façade of the Hanging Church, Babylon.

12. St Anthony the Abbot, the father of monasticism, contemporary mosaic in the court of the Hanging Church, Babylon.

13. The Greek Church of St George built within a Roman tower of the Fort of Babylon.

14. Detail of St George killing the dragon. The Greek Church, Babylon.

Egyptian layer there is an earlier building. The lowest level remains only partially excavated and we do not know with any certainty whether it dates to the Babylonian invasion of Egypt in 664 BC or before.

Babylon was built on a canal that led to the Nile and controlled the river traffic from the eastern Delta to Upper Egypt. The fort included a temple built by Nectanebo II (360-343 BC) and dedicated to the victory of Horus over Seth. Some stones from this temple were found re-used in the masonry of the Gate of Diocletian. They bear reliefs that represent the youthful king as Horus slaying the serpent of Seth, and it is likely that this was how Babylon came to be associated with the story of St George and the dragon in Christian times (fig. 7). The site is now dominated by the Greek Church of St George, and legend has it that the Christian hero was once imprisoned in the fort (figs 13, 14). In the late Roman Period the walls of Babylon presented a formidable defence. The fort could hold up to 5,000 soldiers and its high walls were surrounded by a moat.

Christianity in Egypt followed the Nile south to Upper Egypt. The fourth and fifth centuries were the most fruitful, witnessing the founding of monastic communities in Nitria, Kellia and Scetis (Wadi el Natrun) in the 330s, as well as the emergence of the first monastic leaders, Anthony (251-354, fig. 12), Macarius (300-390), Pachomius (292-346) and Shenouda (385-465). By the end of the fourth century there were almost a hundred bishops in Egypt.

Many ancient temples were converted into monastic centres. Deir (= monastery) el Medina and Deir el Bahari in the Theban necropolis came to be occupied by Christian monks who built churches within the ancient walls. One of the earliest Christian buildings in Egypt was placed between the birth-house and the coronation-house of the temple of Hathor at Dendera. Some of the blocks from the birth-house were re-used in the new construction. The church became a famous Christian centre; Jerome described an assembly of 50,000 monks celebrating Easter at Dendera.[3] The second court of the temple of Ramses III at Medinet Habu was also converted into a church. Its wall reliefs were covered with clay, plastered in stucco and painted with Christian themes.

Pilgrims came from all over Christendom to visit the monasteries of Egypt. The tomb of St Menas near Lake Mariut, outside Alexandria, enjoyed special popularity – St Menas was believed to be a healer. Rufinus (380-401) described a meeting of 10,000 monks in Arsinoe in the Fayoum Oasis. The same figure was quoted by Palladius, a historian of fourth-century monasticism. He also mentioned twelve convents for women at Arsinoe. The bishop of Bahnasa estimated the number of monks in Middle Egypt at 10,000 and nuns at 20,000, living in 40 monasteries and convents. Archaeological evidence has revealed a great monastic settlement in the Kharga Oasis in the Western Desert, dating to the fourth century. The necropolis of the monastery at Bhagawat contains over 200 chapels. Wadi el Natrun had 50 monasteries and over 5,000 monks. East of Wadi Natrun,

15. Painted funerary shroud showing the deceased, whose portrait
has been added separately, flanked by Osiris and Anubis, the ancient
Egyptian gods of the Afterlife, second century, tempera on linen. The
Pushkin Museum of Fine Arts, Moscow.

16. Portrait of a man, 160-180, encaustic on wood. The Metropolitan Museum of Art, New York.

17. Portrait of a lady; the golden wreath symbolizes apotheosis, 90-120, encaustic on wood. The Metropolitan Museum of Art, New York.

18. Coptic funerary stele showing the deceased in Christian prayer
with the ancient Egyptian gods Horus and Anubis on either side, sixth
century, limestone. National Museum, Alexandria.

19. Coptic funerary stele with the Christian symbols of the cross, the shell and the vine, and two ancient Egyptian lotus columns symbolizing rebirth, sixth century, sandstone. National Museum, Alexandria.

at Kellia, 750 hermitages were built in the fifth century. This site was described by many early Christian writers, among them Palladius and Rufinus.

Burial remains indicate that mummification remained common until the fourth century. Mummies were covered with funeral shrouds decorated with scenes from the ancient Egyptian religion; a portrait panel of the deceased in the prime of life, painted on wood or cartonnage, was inserted in the mummy-wrappings over the face (fig. 15). The artistic style was in the best classical tradition, the symbols Egyptian. Since the oldest mummies of this type were discovered in the Fayoum Oasis, the portrait panels are often called Fayoum portraits, although finds come from all over Egypt (figs 16, 17).

From the beginning of the fourth century onwards, mummification went out of fashion. Burials began to follow Christian customs and tombs were marked with stelae carved in stone. Images of the ancient gods of the afterlife remained popular and were often combined with Christian prayers; in fact, it is not unusual to find ancient Egyptian, Classical and Christian symbols side by side until the sixth century and the arrival of the Arabs (figs 18, 19).

The first bishops of the see of Alexandria, which would later become the Coptic Orthodox Church, are only names on a list; virtually nothing is known about them. The first great figures of the Church in Egypt were scholars rather than bishops, directors of the Catechetical School of Alexandria: Clement (160-215) and Origen (185-251). Both were versed in Greek philosophy and their lives' work was one of great integration: they transformed Christianity from a localized cult for the poorest class into a fully-fledged religion with a philosophy and a cosmology.

Christianity in Egypt did not grow either regularly or systematically. The Gnostic Christians (from Greek *gnosis*, 'knowledge') Basilides, Valentinus and Carpocrates were more popular in Alexandria than the scholars of the Catechetical School. Many of their writings were destroyed during the orthodox purges of the fourth century, and little is known about the Gnostic communities. A chance discovery has revealed twelve Gnostic codices hidden in a jar in Nag el Hammadi in Upper Egypt.[4] They vary widely in content and point to a wide spectrum of influences: the Old and New Testaments, Greek and Roman mystery cults, Persian mysticism. They can be described as a microcosm of a pluralistic society that reflects Egypt's diverse population living together and sharing beliefs that had merged into a syncretic alliance. This heritage was slowly and systematically destroyed by the orthodox Copts, who objected to the foreign and pagan influences corrupting their nation and faith.

The Coptic Church of Egypt was fiercely nationalist. The Copts had opposed the Roman rule of their country from the very start. The monks, rooted as they were in the Egyptian desert and countryside, openly voiced their resentment of oppressive foreign rule and Greek cultural hegemony

20. The Monastery of St
Anthony in the Eastern
Desert.

21. St Catherine's
Monastery, Sinai Peninsula.

22. Two archangels in the arch of a doorway, twelfth-century fresco painting. Monastery of St Anthony in the Eastern Desert.

23. A monk in the Monastery of St Paul in the Eastern Desert.

centred in Alexandria. Roman persecutions of Christians did not help. The Great Persecution under Diocletian in 284 caused the deaths of thousands. So harsh is the Coptic recollection of Diocletian's rule that they still use the Calendar of the Martyrs as the beginning of the New Era. It begins its count in AD 284 in commemoration of those who died for their faith at the hands of the Romans. Anthony the Abbot was born in 251 during the Decian persecution, and later went to Alexandria to confess his faith during the Great Persecution of Diocletian. Monasticism had its roots in the heroic Christianity demonstrated by scores of nameless Egyptian martyrs (figs 20, 22, 23).

From the rule of Constantine onwards things became worse, not better. Greek-speaking Christians, close to the Church of Constantinople, came to be designated 'Melkites' ('the emperor's men'). Coptic-speaking Christians saw them as harbouring foreign sympathies and opposed them at every turn. This stubborn, bitter division caused the two sides to take opposing stands at all the Church Councils, from Nicaea to Chalcedon. It was against this background that relations with Constantinople unfolded.

In Alexandria, heated disputes on the nature of Christianity caused the struggle to become ever more virulent. The first Church Council, convened by Constantine in 325 at Nicaea, was occasioned by an Alexandrian dispute between the presbyter Arius and Bishop Alexander. It established the precedent of imperial intervention in imposing church dogma. The Council of Constantinople, convened in 381, had far-reaching effects for Egypt: it declared that the bishop of Constantinople was second only to the bishop of Rome and officially undermined the primacy of Alexandria. The riots that followed in Alexandria were so violent that the Catechetical School, which had remained a force in the intellectual life of the city for nearly two centuries, was destroyed.[5] From then on, the patriarchs of Alexandria fought to maintain their position in relation to Constantinople, but the breach had become too wide.

One more heresy sprang up in Alexandria – Monophysitism, the belief in the single nature of Christ; it is still upheld by the Coptic and Ethiopian Churches. The first Monophysite was Patriarch Dioscuros, the official founder of the Coptic Church. His teaching was condemned at the Council of Chalcedon and Dioscuros was exiled in 451. Chalcedon signalled the Byzantine determination to exert authority over Egypt and Egypt's equal determination not to submit to pressure. Ostensibly the point of conflict was one of doctrine. But in reality the Church of Egypt wanted to separate from both the Byzantine and the Latin Churches. There is little doubt that the precedence of the sees of Constantinople and Rome over the see of Alexandria had everything to do with Egypt's refusal to accept any doctrinal modification. The opposition to the Melkites became the latest episode in a long struggle for independence that was political as well as religious in nature. The Church became a medium through which long brewing racial tensions and social differences were loudly voiced.[6]

2. Christianity in Egypt

After the Council of Chalcedon, which the Copts rejected, the way was paved for the Coptic Church to establish itself as a separate entity. The main centre of learning for the Coptic Church became the Monastery of St Macarius in Wadi el Natrun. No longer even spiritually linked to Constantinople, theologians began to write in Coptic, abandoning the use of Greek. Coptic art developed its own national character and the Copts stood united against the imperial power.

The divided nature of the Church in Egypt was also reflected in the monasteries. The Pachomian monastery of Metanoia at Canopus in the Delta had Melkite leanings while the Pachomian monasteries in Upper Egypt remained staunchly Coptic. The monastic community of Kellia, west of the Nile Delta, physically illustrates the schism between the Melkites and the Copts. Before 451 and the Council of Chalcedon Kellia had one church. After 451, it had two: one for each side of the Chalcedonian schism. Kellia had become a community divided against itself. After the Council of Chalcedon there were essentially two Churches in Egypt, often with two opposing patriarchs, one Greek and the other Coptic. This religious civil war enervated the country, leaving it weak and exposed at the time of the Arab conquest in 641.

3

The Arian Dispute

In the fourth century, an Alexandrian dispute on the nature of Christianity shook up the Christian communities all over the Eastern Empire. It began when a presbyter called Arius clashed with the Melkite bishop Alexander on the central problem of Christian teaching: the relationship of God the father to Jesus Christ, his son. Arius believed that Jesus was not one with the father, but a distinct presence in his own right. He backed his view with citations from Proverbs and from the New Testament where Jesus claimed to be distinct from his father. What clinched the matter for many Christians was the suffering of Christ, so vividly portrayed in the gospels. Arius believed it was designed to show his human side and when he challenged Alexander about the nature of the trinity, he thought that he was representing a theological position cogently justified and backed by the scriptures. To Alexander this position implied that Christ was somehow a lesser divinity, a doctrine he called 'subordination'. The dispute reached dramatic proportions when Arius interrupted one of Alexander's sermons and Alexander had him excommunicated.

The matter was brought to the attention of the emperor Constantine. At first, Constantine thought it was a non-issue. He composed a letter to Arius and Alexander in which he called their speculations 'idle and trivial', and appealed to their duty to 'maintain the spirit of concord'.[1] He had no time for it; his agenda required that consensus be maintained and that Christians be brought under the umbrella of the state.[2] But neither side was willing to give up. Furthermore, the controversy had become widespread − the bishop of every see in eastern Christendom had aligned himself with one side or the other. Constantine had to act if he was to achieve any stable support from the eastern Christian communities. In 316 he had granted special favours to the Christian clergy in an attempt to tie them to the service of the state, exempting them from paying tax and from civic duty. He soon discovered that his political position was seriously threatened by the endemic disunity of the Greek-speaking Christians in the east. The number and diversity of communities calling themselves Christian was so vast that he had to face the dilemma whether to give patronage to all of them or to privilege some over others. Constantine's solution was practical: he called on Eusebius, the most learned and lucid of the eastern bishops, to draw up a creed; then he called a council of bishops at which he planned to enforce it.

In 325 every Greek-speaking bishop was summoned to discuss the controversy at the imperial palace in Nicaea. As such discussions had largely bypassed the Latin-speaking Christians, the bishop of Rome was required to send only observers.[3] Constantine opened the council with a speech in Latin, reinforcing the distance between himself and the Greek-speaking participants.[4] He stressed his determination to encourage a consensus and reminded the Churches that they depended on him for patronage. If they settled the controversy, they would be 'acting in a manner most pleasing to the supreme God and they would confer an exceeding favour on their fellow servant, the emperor'. All he wanted was peace.

Then Eusebius read his document; it was conciliatory in tone and tried to avoid many issues raised by Arius. However, it opposed the position of Arius and ended with a number of anathemas condemning specific Arian beliefs. It is not entirely clear why the council rounded so emphatically on Arius. The most likely explanation is that Constantine sensed that the majority of the bishops opposed Arius and tried to capitalize on the council's mood.

It was not an easy victory; many of the bishops had to be pressured to consent. But dependent as they were on Constantine for patronage, they were not able to resist him. After obtaining a majority for the new creed, Constantine commanded that Arius be excommunicated and exiled, along with two of his closest supporters who refused to sign.

In the short term, no one seems to have taken the council or its creed seriously. Other than Arius and the exiled bishops 'all the rest saluted the emperor, signed the formula and went on teaching as they always had'.[5] Constantine himself realized that his enforced creed did nothing to maintain the allegiance of the Greek-speaking Christians. He sought reconciliation with the Arians, personally receiving Arius and reassigning the two exiled bishops to their sees. He then demanded that Alexander reinstate Arius, but Alexander refused and died in the interim. When Alexander's successor Athanasius also refused, Constantine had him exiled to Gaul. In 335 Constantine summoned Arius to Constantinople and ordered the bishops to admit him to communion. The day before the service Arius died rather dramatically of a haemorrhage in a public latrine in Constantinople. Rumours circulated he had been poisoned, though no one could point to the culprit with any certainty.

Within ten years after the Council of Nicaea all the leading supporters of the Nicene creed had been demoted, exiled from their sees or otherwise disgraced. No bishops gained lasting status for signing up; on the contrary, they were disposed of by the emperor. Among the bishops only Athanasius continued to support Nicaea, the others ignored it. To all appearances, the Nicene creed was dead. Had not the issue been raised again in the 350s, it would have been no more than a footnote in history.

After the death of Constantine in 337, his three surviving sons, Constantine II, Constans and Constantius, quickly eliminated other members of their family and divided the empire between them. Constantine II was killed when he tried to invade the territory of Constans; the latter was executed in a palace coup by Magnentius, who was in turn defeated by Constantius in a battle in Gaul in 351. Constantius remained sole ruler for the next ten years.

For the Church, trying to adapt to its new role as a religion sponsored by the State, it was a particularly difficult time. The issue requiring immediate attention was how to come up with a doctrine that would bring some form of order to the Christian communities. If Constantius was to continue exempting the Christian clergy from tax, it was imperative to clear up the issue of who was who in the Church hierarchy, and that called for tightening up Christian doctrine. Constantine's law of 336 explicitly stated: 'The benefits that have been granted in consideration of religion must benefit only the adherents of the Catholic (meaning 'universally accepted, correct') faith. It is our will, moreover, that heretics and schismatics shall not only be alien to those privileges, but shall be bound and subjected to various compulsory public services.' The definition of Catholicism and heresy took on a new urgency.

The issue was still a matter of debate because Nicaea had solved nothing. The debates entered a period of confusion as personal rivalries became entangled with theoretical arguments. Accusations of heresy and fraud flew across the empire.

Like his father, Constantius was determined to find a workable solution. He assembled a number of eastern bishops sympathetic to Nicaea and had them draft four documents, known as the Sirmian creeds (from their being issued at the imperial city of Sirmium in the Balkans).[6] In 359 Constanius adopted the fourth Sirmian creed, called the Dated creed, as a rallying ground for consensus. He then called two councils, one in the west at Arminium (Rimini) and another in the east at Seleucia.

Things did not go smoothly. The western council proved highly suspicious of 'the eastern doctrine' and revived the straightforward formula of Nicaea. A delegation of ten bishops then travelled to Thrace, but after discussions with the eastern bishops, the delegates changed their minds and persuaded a reconvened Arminium to accept the Dated creed, arguing that they would be out of step with the eastern bishops if they refused. A consensus of eastern bishops in Seleucia was then persuaded not to be out of step with the western bishops. Finally, Constantius called a joint council in 360 in Constantinople with delegations from the two earlier councils, at which he officially pronounced the Dated creed as canon and declared all others to be heretical. It was disseminated throughout the empire as an imperial edict.

The history of Christianity now took an unexpected turn. Constantius had appointed one of the few surviving members of his family, his cousin Julian, Caesar in the western provinces. Julian had proved to be a fine general. In 360 the troops had hailed him Augustus, to the fury of Constantius, who hurried back from the Persian border to confront him. When Constantius died unexpectedly in 361, Julian found himself sole emperor.

Julian had been brought up a Christian and even served as lector; but according to the historian Ammianus Marcellinus, he had been put off by the vicious infighting among Christians. As Marcellinus put it: 'Experience had taught him that no wild beasts are so dangerous to man as Christians are to one another.' The roots for his distaste may have been caused by the brutal murder of his family by the three surviving sons of Constantine, who were Christian emperors. Whatever his reasons, once he had buried Constantius with suitable piety, Julian adopted the pagan religion as his own. Summoning the bishops, he ordered them 'to allow every man to practise his belief boldly without hindrance', took away the tax exemption privilege of the Christian clergy and in 362 forbade Christians to teach. He even began rebuilding the Jewish temple in Jerusalem, professing respect for all religions. In the end, during a battle against Sassanid Persia, the pagan emperor was killed by an unknown spear. Everyone suspected the Christians and no one could prove it. One way or another Julian had been eliminated and with his death the house of Constantine came to an end.

The army in the east now proclaimed a staff officer by the name of Jovian emperor, but he died eight months later, just as the army had to cede great portions of Byzantine territory to the Persians. He was followed by Valentinian, who successfully defended (for the last time) the northern borders. Valentinian's brother Valens was appointed co-emperor and when Valentinian died in 375, Valens and his son Gratian became co-emperors (though the army also proclaimed Valentinian II, a son from another marriage, Augustus).

Then disaster struck. In 378, the Huns, a new tribe form the east, had migrated across the eastern border, driving the Goths before them; a mass of refugees had poured across the Danube frontier. The Goths began rampaging across Thrace and confronted Valens at Adrianople, winning a stunning victory: the emperor and 10,000 Byzantine soldiers were killed.

The other co-emperor, Gratian, made the experienced general Theodosius his fellow Augustus, but both of them proved unable to push the Goths back across the border. In the eyes of the army, these rulers had allowed a substantial group of armed men without any allegiance to Rome to settle within the empire and as a consequence, in 383, Gratian was murdered by his own troops. Theodosius became emperor.

Theodosius was of Spanish background and not a Christian. In Thessalonika he became severely ill and while still in bed, he was baptized by the staunchly pro-Nicene bishop of Thessalonika, Acholius.[7] Theodosius then felt better and made his way to Constantinople. When he entered the city he was greeted with seething anger: the *Homoian*[8] clergy established by Constantius after the settlement of 360 and promoted by Valens stood to lose their tax exemption. Gregory of Nysa described the mood in the capital as follows: 'If you ask for change, the man launches into a theological discussion about begotten and unbegotten, if you enquire about the price of bread, the answer is given that the father is greater and the son subordinate, if you remark that the bath is nice, the attendant pronounces that the son is from non-existence.'[9]

In January 381 Theodosius issued an imperial decree declaring the doctrine of the trinity orthodox and expelling the old clergy from their churches. During the same year he called a council of 150 bishops from the east, whose first act was to remove bishop Demophilus and install Gregory of Nazianzus as the new bishop. According to Gregory himself, the council was chaotic; nevertheless, it proceeded to affirm a creed based on Nicene principles (no record of it survives, only a reference made to it at the Council of Chalcedon in 451, where it appears to have been read twice; for a translation of the text see the Appendix). On the final day of the council a new imperial edict was issued and that was the moment when the Nicene formula became part of the official state religion. After that, little room was left for theological discussion.

The emperor's actions may have been caused by several factors, among them the need to control the number of those able to claim tax exemption, and the desire to regroup and unite the citizens of the empire after the disastrous defeat at Adrianople. Theodosius had fought the Goths first hand and he may have felt that the empire was under threat from outside forces. Perhaps he saw orthodoxy as a focus of loyalty to the state. Finally, like Constantine and Constantius before him, he may have seen no alternative except to bend the Church to the will of the emperor. Whatever his reasons, the Nicene formula had changed everything – the assumption that there could be such a thing as doctrinal certainty marked a turning point in western history.

The elevation of Jesus to the status of absolute divinity underpinned the belief of Arius that only a lesser being would have undergone the agony of doubt and suffering on the cross. It appeared to many as the abandonment of the scriptures. Now that the doctrine of the trinity had been proclaimed, the scriptures had to be reinterpreted to defend it. On the one hand, it led to a transformation of the image of Christ in both doctrine and art: he became omnipotent, abstract and remote. On the other, it caused all other Christian communities to go undercover and secretly continue practising their true beliefs.

By adopting the mantle of Christianity and bending the Church to their will, Byzantine emperors began to rule as absolute monarchs. Byzantium achieved political stability, but the price was great. The decree of Theodosius had legitimized the persecution of all those who had different beliefs: Christians, Jews and pagans alike.

Hypatia and St Catherine

In 381 Theodosius issued the decree of orthodoxy; in 385 he strengthened the existing legislation against pagan sacrifices; in 391 he forbade non-Christian ceremonies in Rome and Egypt, and in 392 he outlawed all forms of pagan worship, public and private, throughout the empire. This increasing religious intolerance alarmed the Alexandrians.

In the early years of Theodosius Alexandria was a multicultural centre of learning. The pagan temples were open, Jews attended the rabbinical school and the Museion had its own scholars. The prestigious position of director was held by the astronomer and mathematician Theon, who had produced commentaries on Euclid's *Elements, Data* and *Optics* and on Claudius Ptolemy's *Almagest* and *Handy Tables*.

After the imperial decree of 392 the spiritual life of the city began to unravel. At hearing the news that pagan worship was forbidden, the city's pagan population panicked. In an act of desperation a group of prominent citizens barricaded themselves inside the temple of Serapis on the hill. Among them were three pagan priests and two poets. As news of their incarceration spread around the city street fights broke out. Pagans were attacking Christian converts, black-robed bearded monks exchanging blows with clean-shaven Egyptian priests in white tunics. When Theodosius heard of this running battle he ordered the governor and military commander to intervene.

Byzantine soldiers surrounded the Serapeum and ordered the people who had barricaded themselves inside to leave. As the Egyptian priests and their sympathizers were being led out, the Christian mob flooded in. Frenzied hands grasped the statue of Serapis, dragged it out on the street and smashed it to pieces; this was how the celebrated statue of the sculptor Bryaxis ended its reign.

Then the mob poured into the Daughter Library. Scrolls, manuscripts, maps, books that took centuries to collect, were taken outside, torn to shreds and thrown on a bonfire. Within hours the building and its possessions had been ravaged. The poet Palladas, one of those who had barricaded themselves in protest, remarked: 'where books are being burned, people will burn too'. Those who took part in the defence of the Serapeum were deprived of their positions; most fled to Rome.[1]

In a dramatic reversal of fortune, Christian bishops were suddenly brought to the forefront of power. Only 50 years beforehand they had risked arrest and contempt at the hands of pagan emperors; now they

stood side by side with the local governor (*augustalis*) and military commander (*dux*). So long as they upheld the orthodox creed they could enjoy
status, power and financial support. Many profited from this turn of
events. The Coptic bishop Athanasius was accused of selling in the private
markets of Alexandria grain sent to him by the emperor to distribute to
the poor. His tainted reputation did not prevent him from dislodging one
Christian faction by transferring tax exemption privileges to achieve his
purpose.

His successor Theophilus diverted money given to him to buy shirts for
the poor to finance a building project. Like Athanasius, Theophilus depended on being seen as the champion of orthodoxy to keep his position.
In 402 he condemned the first Alexandrian theologian Origen as a heretic.
During the rule of Theophilus a wave of destruction swept Egypt. Tombs
were ravaged, walls of ancient monuments scraped and statues toppled.
All traces of the ancient world were being systematically obliterated.

After the death of Theophilus two candidates laid claim to succeed him,
his nephew Cyril and the archdeacon Timothy. An election campaign
followed: Timothy appears to have had the backing of the Church and the
military commander. But Cyril gathered the mob of Alexandria and encouraged them to riot for three days. When everyone grew tired, the
triumphant Cyril was installed as bishop. It was the beginning of his reign
of terror.

The first act of the new bishop was to recruit shock troops – *parabolans*
– zealous young men who obediently served his needs. Nominally, their
duty was to help ill and destitute Christians to find a place in almshouses
and hospitals. Already under the last two bishops the *parabolans* had been
transformed into a veritable private army numbering 800. They came to
be viewed with such terror by the population of Alexandria that the
Byzantine emperor himself had to ask that their number be limited to 500.

Cyril set out to conquer the city by force, armed with imperial decrees.
He converted the shrine of St John on Serapeum Hill into the headquarters of the *parabolans*. His first target was the Novatian sect. They
followed the teaching of the Roman priest Novatian who had split from the
official Catholic Church because he found it too lax in readmitting former
Christians who had renounced their faith in the face of persecution. The
Novatians called themselves 'the pure' and adhered to strict self-disci-
pline. Cyril found them too religious; he closed up their churches and
confiscated their furnishings; then he stripped the Novatian bishop of his
possessions.

Next, Cyril turned to the Jews. He found them not religious enough and
criticized them for not observing the Sabbath, so he banned them from
visiting the theatres on Saturdays. As he had no official jurisdiction over
the Jewish community, the elders decided to ignore him. In response, Cyril
posted *parabolans* in theatres throughout the city to prevent Jews from
going in on Saturdays. On one occasion, when the governor Orestes was

giving a speech in a public theatre on Saturday, a brawl broke out when Cyril's agent Hierax began harassing some Jews in the audience. Orestes had Hierax arrested. Cyril then summoned the Jewish elders and warned them to stay away from his agents. His patronizing tone so enraged the elders that a few jumped up and began fighting Cyril's bodyguard. Another brawl ensued; it had to be broken up by soldiers.

This episode started a war. Jewish radicals reacted and a group of angry Jewish youths set an ambush in a newly built Christian church. During the night, some of them began shouting that the church was on fire; Christians from the neighbourhood jumped out of their beds, ran to the church and were set upon by the young men. A bloody fight broke out and many were killed on both sides. Now Cyril had his martyrs. He gathered his troops and set them to loot Jewish sites. He wrote a letter to the emperor complaining about the behaviour of the Jews and proposed to have them expelled from the city.

At this point, the governor Orestes became incensed. The Jewish population had lived in Alexandria from the city's inception. It had always played a vital part in the city's commerce. Alexandria was the home of distinguished philosophers, of the *Septuagint*, the Greek translation of the Old Testament, which was read by the apostles. Orestes wrote a letter to the emperor complaining about Cyril's intrusion into civil matters. The emperor left both letters unanswered; the matter may have been low on his list of priorities.

Cyril made an attempt at reconciliation. He had a meeting with Orestes and appeared ready to establish a truce. But when Orestes reminded him that he was overstepping the boundaries of his power, Cyril pulled the gospels from his sleeve and waved them under the nose of Orestes: God had given him power! Orestes had his guards escort Cyril from the building and Cyril was gravely offended.

Cyril called on the monks of the monastery of Wadi el Natrun, known for their radical views, to show him support. Some 500 monks immediately volunteered to help the Christian bishop and headed for the streets of Alexandria; there, they looked for Orestes and found him riding in his carriage. They surrounded the carriage and began shouting abuse: foreigner, traitor, pagan idolater! Their fanatical hatred so frightened Orestes that he protested he was an Alexandrian and a Christian baptized by Bishop Atticus of Constantinople. At this, one of the monks picked up a rock and threw it at Orestes. It struck him on the head and knocked him down; blood poured over his face. The monks attacked the governor's guards, a fight broke out and the guards fled. Orestes was saved by people who happened to be walking by.

The following day Orestes ordered the arrest of the monk who had thrown the rock; he was duly taken and tortured to death. Two more letters were dispatched to the emperor in Constantinople, one from Orestes, another from Cyril. Orestes complained about the monks' criminal behaviour, Cyril about the 'martyred' monk. Both went unanswered; the emperor did nothing.

It was in this highly charged atmosphere that the story of Hypatia unfolded. She was the daughter of Theon, the Museum director, and a renowned mathematician herself. Most of her life had been spent in the safe haven of the museum. From childhood she had collaborated with her father and had edited his work; she was mentioned as the editor of Theon's commentary on the *Almagest*. According to the philosopher Damascius, Hypatia was 'by nature more refined and talented than her father'. She was a superb mathematician, known for having written a commentary on the notoriously complicated *Algebra* of Diophantus. It is thanks to her that this work, crucial in the development of modern mathematics, survived at all. In what everyone feared were the last days of Hellenism, Hypatia had attracted a following of her own. She gave regular lectures on ethics, astronomy, mathematics and philosophy. Her disciples included the Syrian landowner Olympius, the grammarian Theodosius, the aristocrat Synesius of Cyrene and many other prominent Alexandrians. At least half of her students were Christians, and this may explain why she was left alone by Bishop Theophilus. After the unfortunate episode at the Serapeum (where some of the main protagonists had been close associates of her father Theon) Hypatia continued teaching unhindered. In fact, she might have survived even now had she not decided to show open support for Orestes when he was assaulted.

At the time Orestes was attacked, Hypatia was about 60 years old. It seems that in the new climate she had stopped gathering her circle for fear of Cyril's reprisals; there is a surviving letter of Synesius, written from his estate in Cyrene, in which he bitterly complains about her withdrawal and silence. John of Nikiu described how one day Cyril passed by her house and was overcome with jealousy when he saw a large crowd gathering to hear her speak. She was aware of his animosity. She was also widely respected, had close connections in the government and counted men from the imperial court among her pupils. Her only weakness was that she was not a Christian herself. And this was the weapon that Cyril decided to use.

Cyril began circulating rumours that Hypatia was 'a sorceress, devoted at all times to magic, astrolabes and instruments of music'.[2] She ignored him; in fact, no one in Alexandria paid any attention, and Cyril had to resort to his *parabolans*. He called on a man called Peter, a lector in a church, and commanded him to lead the zealot troops, calling on his sacred duty to eliminate the pagans. As Peter and the young men in black ominously walked through the streets looking for Hypatia, an angry mob gathered behind them. They found Hypatia riding in a chariot outside the Caesareum. The mob surrounded the chariot, dragged her out and stripped her naked. Then they took her inside the temple and tore her body limb from limb. Her mutilated remains were carried outside the walls and burned on a bonfire like those of a witch.

4. Hypatia and St Catherine

After this act of savagery Orestes disappears from history: he may have fled the city. Some councillors wrote to the emperor, but nothing came of it. Cyril had by now his measure of the emperor. The only response from Constantinople was to restrict the number of the *parabolans* and to rest their recruitment with the civil governor, a rule Cyril quickly overturned. Although Hypatia was assassinated for political reasons, by 418 Cyril had succeeded in portraying her death as a fight between Christians and pagans. John of Nikiu summed up Cyril's intention in the following sentence: 'All the people surrendered to Cyril and named him "the new Theophilus" for destroying the last remains of idolatry in the city.'[3]

Hypatia's legend still lives; it has inspired dozens of plays, poems and novels. Even two feminist academic journals have taken on her name. In the middle ages her tragic story was preserved in the myth of St Catherine of Alexandria, martyred at the wheel after refuting 50 philosophers who tried to persuade her against her faith. In Freudian fashion she was appropriated by the Christian Church and became the patron of St Catherine's monastery on Sinai with its great library and collection of icons (fig. 21).

Hypatia's death was just another rung on the ladder of Cyril's career. He now turned his attention to the rival bishop of Constantinople, Nestorius, and accused him of being a heretic for his view about the two natures of Christ. After having manipulated a council held at Ephesus to uphold his claim, Cyril had to convince emperor Theodosius II to support him. This involved massive bribery. The sum of 77,760 gold pieces, tapestries, carpets, even ostrich eggs, were made available for distribution, with double handouts to those who opposed Cyril. The strategy worked; Nestorius was deposed and sent into exile, and in 435 Theodosius ordered the burning of all his writings.

Thus, by tying the bishops into the imperial administration and giving them access to wealth and status, Constantine and his successors achieved a major political transformation from which there would be no turning back. The balance of power between Church and State had shifted to such a degree that more determined bishops were even prepared to assert Church authority over the State.

Cyril's episcopate lasted for nearly 32 years; he was remembered as a doctor of the Church and even raised to sainthood. In reality, he had done irreparable damage to the city's ethnic fabric and all but annihilated its long intellectual tradition. During his 30 years as bishop, ethnic intolerance decimated the city's multicultural communities. Greeks and Jews left in large numbers; academic life became extinct. After Theon and Hypatia we no longer hear of the Museion or its activities. Alexandria finally succumbed to the only real enemy of life: fear.

What remained of the books from the Great Library was hidden. The original collection of 700,000 volumes had been damaged in several incidents: during the fire set by the soldiers of Julius Caesar in the civil war of 48 BC; in the destruction of the city centre by the soldiers of Caracalla in AD 215; in the demolition of the Royal Quarter by Aurelian's soldiers after the rebellion of 273; during the battering of the city by Diocletian's army in response to the rebellion of 297; and when the Daughter Library was burned in the aftermath of the standoff at the Serapeum in 392.

We know that after the demolition of the royal quarter by Aurelian's army in 273 the remaining books were distributed around several buildings in the city. The greatest body, stored in the Daughter Library, was destroyed in 392. Yet it would appear that several other collections survived destruction and went underground. During Cyril's reign of terror possession of pagan and heretical books could mean death at the hands of the *parabolans*, and those who wanted to read did so in secret and in the privacy of their homes. This was how private libraries came into being.

We have evidence of their existence from the pen of John Moschus, a Greek monk of Syrian origin, who travelled to Alexandria with his pupil and friend Sophronius in the sixth century. They were driven from Syria in 605 during the wars of Phocas and spent almost ten years in Alexandria, reading, writing and making frequent excursions to the monasteries around the city. Both scholars were friends of the Melkite patriarch John the Almoner. All three fled from Alexandria at the time of the Persian invasion.

John described two book collections, one belonging to Theodore the Philosopher and the other to Zoilus the Reader, both poor men who possessed 'nothing but a mantle and a number of books'. Theodore studied philosophy at home while Zoilus practised the art of illuminating manuscripts. John also described a certain Cosmas the Student who 'possessed the finest private library in Alexandria and freely lent his books to all readers. He was very poor, and the whole of his house, which was full of books, contained no furniture, but a bed and a table. His library was open to all comers. Every reader could ask for the book he wanted, and there read it. Day by day I visited Cosmas and it is mere fact that I never once entered his house without finding him engaged either in reading, or in writing.'[4] When pressed to answer how long he had been living like this, Cosmas answered that he had spent 33 years reading books in his house.

One more reference to a private library in Alexandria is found in the *Chronicle* of Zachariah of Mytilene. Zachariah mentioned that the Syrian bishop Moro Bar Kustant, exiled from Syria to Alexandria in the first half of the sixth century, had acquired 'a library containing admirable books, in which is found abundance of great profit for those who love knowledge'.[5] After Moro's death the books were transferred to the treasury of the Church of Amida in Syria.[6] Not only had the city become a haven for private book collectors, but the export of books was not forbidden.

The school of astronomy, mathematics and mechanics also survived Cyril's purges. In the sixth century a scholar by the name of Stephen wrote several books on astronomy and geography and provided newly acquired information about the 'Eastern Seas'. Their survey had been made by the explorer Cosmas, nicknamed Indicopleustes (the Indian navigator), a merchant adventurer from Alexandria, whose love of travel and discovery had prompted him to make long scientific voyages around Arabia and India. Though Cosmas had died some time before Stephen wrote the book, his works were still available and much valued.[7] Stephen was also credited with writing a book on astrology in which he predicted the coming of Islam.

There was one more philosopher worthy of mention, John Philoponus. He had pursued many branches of learning and some of his notes on Aristotle are still extant. He argued against Aristotle's system of natural observation, countering him with his own personal experiments in physics. He was the precursor of Galileo when he proposed that falling objects were guided by another force than their weight, as Aristotle thought. But John was the last of his kind; no one in Europe practised this sort of analysis of nature until the fourteenth century.

The closing of the Platonic Academy in Athens by Justinian in 529 brought a definitive end to the Hellenistic tradition. The deaths of Stephen and John Philoponus and the closing of the Athenian academies had come in the same decade. For about 300 years after this time scholarly activity was largely confined to monasteries and almost entirely devoted to theological and ecclesiastic matters. There was nothing that could be described as philosophy in Europe until the reforms of Charlemagne at the end of the eighth century.

As late as 680 Alexandria still remained a centre of learning. Barhebreus (Abu el Faraj) described how James of Edessa went there to improve his study of the Greek language and the scriptures.[8] But cut off from its classical past, the city was simply adrift. The Royal and Jewish Quarters had long been abandoned and the Museion and the tomb of Alexander lay in ruins. After the despotic reigns of Theophilus and Cyril the city led an intimidated existence. Commerce was kept up, but with the rise of Constantinople supremacy over the Mediterranean Sea was lost. Books were hidden, science and learning waned. Christian communities clustered around the Caesareum and the Serapeum, both of which had now become churches. The great Caesareum, built by Cleopatra in honour of Julius Caesar and dedicated to Saturn, was rededicated to St Michael, as his feast day coincided with the feast of Saturn.[9] According to Eutychius, the bronze statue of Saturn was melted and made into a large cross. The Church of St John on Serapeum Hill continued to function as the headquarters of the *parabolans*. Alexandria was up for grabs.

5

The Persian Conquest

In 614 the Persians invaded Syria. They encountered determined resistance by the people of Syria and it took them an entire year to overrun the country and reach Jerusalem. When they took Jerusalem they slaughtered the inhabitants, plundered the treasures and set the city on fire. The Church of the Holy Sepulchre was destroyed and the Holy Cross carried away as plunder. In May of 615 they deported a multitude of Christians into captivity, among them the patriarch of Jerusalem, Zacharias.

Those who escaped after the destruction of Jerusalem fled to Egypt, most of them to Alexandria. The city's population was swollen by crowds of refugees and the resources of the Melkite patriarch John the Almoner were drained. To make matters worse, the following summer brought an exceedingly low Nile flood and a devastating famine. John worked without respite, providing almshouses and hospitals for the ill and wounded, and when two corn-ships from Sicily carrying 40,000 bushels of grain reached Alexandria, he held a thanksgiving mass at the Caesareum.

In the autumn of 616, the Persians advanced on Egypt. Both Pelusium and Babylon surrendered without a battle and after the fall of Memphis the army marched by land to Alexandria. Finding the city gates firmly shut and Alexandria's defensive walls well nigh impregnable, the Persians vented their anger on the surrounding countryside.[1] The monastery of Wadi el Natrun was particularly hard hit, the monks killed, the churches destroyed and the library burnt. The shrine of St Menas was levelled to the ground and only the monasteries of Deir el Kibrius and Ennaton were left undisturbed, probably because of their distance from the Persian camp.[2]

The Byzantine garrisons protecting Alexandria had been considerably weakened by the withdrawal of troops to other parts of the empire as province after province fell into Persian hands. No relief came from emperor Heraclius in Constantinople, the grain traffic was seriously diminished and people felt they would have to surrender for fear of starvation. Even John the Almoner fled to Cyprus and soon afterwards died near the city of his birth, Amathus, on 11 November 617. Times were unsettled, events unfolding fast, and the city appeared to be doomed.

After several months of siege Alexandria fell through treachery. It was revealed to the Persians that there was a poorly guarded entrance to a canal which led to the sea. The canal ran from the western harbour through the city[3] and passed by a bridge under the Canopic Way. The harbour end of this canal was unguarded. The Persians procured a number of fishing boats, filled them with soldiers disguised as fishermen and sent them out to sea in the dead of night. When the boats reached the canal in the morning they shouted the password and entered unhindered. They disembarked, hurried to the Gate of the Moon, killed the guards and opened the gates to the Persian army. Before the alarm could be sounded they proclaimed the victory of Chosroes from the walls. All who could took flight by sea, but unfavourable winds and storms blew the ships back and they were captured. The treasures of the city together with the keys were sent to Chosroes in 618.

Having conquered Alexandria, the Persians spared the inhabitants and only a few were sent to captivity in Persia.[4] Among those who remained unmolested was the new Coptic patriarch Andronicus. With the Melkite patriarch gone, Andronicus had made himself at home in the city. The Persians allowed him to stay, perhaps because his cousin was chairman of the Council of Alexandria and the Persians needed his help to govern the city.

It took the Persians three years to conquer the whole of the Nile Valley down to Syene (Aswan). Evidence from contemporary Coptic chronicles suggests that the Copts, like the Syrians, regarded them with alarm and abhorrence. The *Life* of the Coptic saint Anba Shenouda, written in the seventh century, described the Persian invasion as a time of great sorrow. Another chronicle, written in the seventh century by Bishop Pisentios of Coptos in Upper Egypt,[5] lamented that 'God had abandoned Egypt and delivered the Copts to the nations without mercy'. Having heard of the arrival of 'the fire-worshippers' Pisentios fled with a faithful disciple to the mountainside, where the two of them discovered a square chamber measuring 70 square feet, hollowed out of the rock and supported by six piers of columns. It was the burial place of a few hundred mummies, which had lain undisturbed for centuries. Here Pisentios resolved to live alone, and when his disciple went to fetch water and food he would return to find him in conversation with the mummies, whose faces and names Pisentios knew well. He claimed that one of the mummies talked to him, describing in great detail how they had been laid to rest by the Greeks and lamenting that they had been ignorant of the Christian faith. The mummies were described as 'shrouded in the pure silk of kings'; their names were written out on a scroll. The list was probably written in Greek; the mummies may have been of the Fayoum type (figs 24, 25, 26, 27).

The Persians remained in Egypt for some ten years.[6] There is no record of any resistance to their conquest other than at Alexandria. They imposed a tribute on the Coptic Church and confiscated the endowments of the banished Melkites. Yet, unlike in Jerusalem, churches and civil buildings in Alexandria were left untouched. This may have been because of the distance between Egypt and the Persian homeland. A web of unbridged waterways covered the Egyptian Delta, long stretches of desert lay between Egypt and Syria, and heavy transport from one country to another would have been practically impossible. In the Royal Harbour they built the so-called 'Palace of the Persians' that survived until the Arab conquest (fig. 28).

We have some evidence that during the Persian stay in Egypt the Alexandrian school of medicine was still active. Physicians who had been trained at the school had a great reputation. The court physician in Constantinople was an Alexandrian[7] and Sergius of Rhesaina, head of all the doctors in Babylonia, had also studied there. An Alexandrian priest named Aaron had written 28 medical treatises in Syriac; they were later recorded by Barhebreus and retained great repute among the Arabs.[8] Owing to the presence of a great number of Syrian scholars, all the principal works of medicine were written in Syriac. Syrian scholars were also busy translating the *Septuagint* and the New Testament into Syriac at the Ennaton monastery. In Wadi el Natrun the Syrian Convent (Deir el Suriani) was built and its library re-furnished for students of theology.

The production of textiles, the work of Coptic craftsmen, flourished. The Persians seem to have acquired a taste for Egyptian textiles and Persian designs came into fashion. The materials, looms and dyes were produced at Saqqara, the Fayoum Oasis and Upper Egypt. Textiles were sold in the great markets of Memphis and Alexandria and shipped abroad from ports on the Red Sea. The Copts seem to have settled into a life of tranquillity despite their dislike of the Persians. Perhaps they had no choice but to regard Persian rule as just one more change of master, a situation they had known from time immemorial. The Coptic patriarch Andronicus was left undisturbed in his see and allowed to reside in Alexandria until his death. His successor Benjamin was peaceably elected and passed the first years of his pontificate under the shelter of the Persian government.

The enmity between the Copts and the Melkites persisted. The ancient historian Agathias described how a Byzantine prefect employed fourteen copyists to corrupt the writings of the Coptic fathers, particularly those of Cyril, so that they could be quoted as heretical from published texts. Such frauds exacerbated tensions between the two camps that were soon to explode.

It was in this climate that the early life of Benjamin unfolded. He came from a well-to-do Coptic family of landowners in the Delta. He received his habit at the monastery of Kibrius where he was taught by Theonas. The latter realized that Benjamin was extraordinarily gifted and introduced him to the patriarch Andronicus. Benjamin immediately won the patriarch's fullest confidence; in due course he was ordained into the priesthood and aided Andronicus in the administration of the whole patriarchate. When Andronicus died he nominated Benjamin as his successor.

At this time Benjamin was still quite young, no more than 35 years old.[9] In January 623 he was crowned patriarch, the *pallium* placed in his hands in St Mark's Cathedral. His election was a popular one, he had won both

24. Portrait of a youth with a cruciform flower in the centre of the wreath, *c.* 125-150, encaustic on wood. The Pushkin Museum of Fine Arts, Moscow.

25. Portrait of a youth; the gold of the wreath and the background symbolizes eternal life, *c.* 138-180, encaustic on wood. The Pushkin Museum of Fine Arts, Moscow.

26. Portrait of a young woman, *c.* 130-161, encaustic on wood. The Pushkin Museum of Fine Arts, Moscow.

27. Portrait of a man, *c.* 130-161, encaustic on wood. The Pushkin
Museum of Fine Arts, Moscow.

28. Relief from a building in Alexandria showing a Persian-style hunting motif, sixth century, limestone. National Museum, Alexandria.

the love and the veneration of his people. He retained their confidence unimpaired through all the vicissitudes of what turned out to be the most eventful primacy in Coptic history.

As patriarch, the first act of Benjamin was to restore the unity of the Coptic Church. He was particularly active in checking abuse in those churches where the bishops had lost control in the tumult of war. A visit to the fort of Babylon before his consecration had shocked him and now he distributed a pastoral letter to all the bishops, in which he said: 'During my stay in Helwan and Babylon I saw a number of forward men, both priests and deacons; my soul abhors their works. I write this letter to the bishops bidding them to hold an inquiry once a month concerning everyone in the clergy who has been ordained for less than ten years [i.e. since the Persian conquest].' This letter made it clear that he took his mission seriously, a point he drove home by excommunicating several priests in the diocese of Babylon. When he went on foot from Babylon to bring to account a notorious offender, on whose house he called down fire from heaven, wherever he passed people flocked to receive his benediction. By now he had become a charismatic figure.

The successor of the Melkite patriarch John the Almoner was called George; his nominal appointment took place in Constantinople some time before 621. It is not clear if and when George's appointment was made effective by residence in Alexandria; he may never have set foot in Egypt. The Melkite patriarch could not have expected any welcome from either the Persians or the Copts and his return would have served no purpose until the return of the Byzantine garrisons. George's years in the church archives are somewhat vague, possibly because he died before he could take office.

In his absence Benjamin ruled in peace. Alexandria had been enlivened by rumours about the rising prophet of Mecca, but for the moment everyone found the actions of the emperor Heraclius in Constantinople far more alarming. At Pentapolis, west of Alexandria, a ship had been wrecked, and not just any ship, but one laden with treasures and sent to Carthage by Heraclius. The only explanation for the emperor's desperate act was that he planned to return to Carthage where his career had begun. His fortunes had fallen low and his empire retreated within the walls of Constantinople. From the windows of his own palace Heraclius could see the Persians at Chalcedon on the opposite shore of the Bosporus. On the west side of the city hordes of Huns and Tartars were raiding the countryside and approaching the city gates. It appeared to everyone that Heraclius was giving up. He had asked Chosroes for peace and his request had been disdainfully refused. Now his planned escape suggested that his strength was broken.

With what feeling Benjamin and the Copts received these news it is difficult to imagine. On the one hand, Heraclius was a Christian emperor besieged by non-Christians. On the other, the Persians kept the Melkites in exile while tolerating the Copts. Furthermore, the Copts were Monophysite and staunchly pro-Nicene. At this time Patriarch Sergius of Constantinople had come up with a new doctrine: Monothelism: Christ, while possessing two natures that had been confirmed at Chalcedon, had but a single *will*. It was a new formula designed to satisfy all Christians. As ever, the Coptic Church opposed it. So did the Syrian. Furthermore, with the Melkites in exile the Copts could profess any creed they liked. In many ways the *status quo* was a kind of solution for the Copts and when news reached Alexandria that Heraclius was assembling an army to fight the Persian foe, Egypt remained strangely quiet. Perhaps everyone realized that it was far from the end of the story.

6

Heraclius' Crusade

It was Patriarch Sergius, the architect of Monothelism, who breathed new purpose into Heraclius. Shocked and angered by the news of the emperor's planned escape, Sergius called him to St Sophia and made him take a solemn oath at the high altar that he would be true to the trust vested in him and fight to save Christendom from the enemies of Christ. Then Sergius began delivering a series of fiery sermons about the rescue of the Holy Cross from the infidels. As his words echoed to the four corners of the empire, Heraclius began preparing for war. The emperor's second offer of peace to Chosroes had been refused with a curt reply: 'The Roman Empire belongs to me. Heraclius is a rebel and a slave and I will grant no peace until he abandons the worship of the crucified one for the worship of the sun.'[1] The deliberate insolence of this answer brought the religious aspect of the war to the forefront and fired the indignation of the people.

After this there was no turning back. Heraclius was forced into action: he bought the peace of the Huns and the Tartars, thus securing the landward side of the capital;[2] he enrolled and equipped an army, which together with allies numbered 120,000 men; to obtain funds for the expedition he collected all the gold and silver vessels from the churches to coin into money, a sacrifice to which the clergy in the capital happily consented. While army supplies were being gathered and stored, he trained his men. In the end his military talents (which had secured him the throne in the first place) became obvious to everyone and he became a great inspiration to his soldiers.

When all was ready Heraclius made over the government to his son and named the patriarch Sergius and the patrician Bonus as guardians. Having prepared to strike, he transported his army by sea to Cilicia, a move rendered possible by his great shipping resources and undisputed mastery of the Mediterranean.[3] On Easter Monday of 622 he weighed anchor from Constantinople and sailed south. His armada landed and camped at Issus, the site of Alexander's first victory over the Persians nine centuries before. It was a symbolic and a tactical move: it drove an immediate wedge into the centre of the territory commanded by the Persians. In the following year, another expedition to Trebizond drove in a further wedge from the north side of Asia Minor. The pressure on the Persians now became enormous; as blow followed blow the Persians recalled their armies from Chalcedon and Alexandria. By 627 they had fully withdrawn from the Bosporus and the Nile Valley.

The crowning achievement of the war was Heraclius' capture of Dastagerd in February of 628. Having lost the battle Chosroes escaped, but he was caught and put to death by his own men. His palace was set on fire, his treasures taken. Numerous captives from Syria and Egypt were freed, among them the patriarch Zacharias of Jerusalem. The relic of the Holy Cross was found unharmed and delivered into the emperor's hands. The war was concluded by a treaty of peace.

On 15 May 628 the victory of Heraclius was announced from the great gallery of St Sophia. Church bells rang throughout the capital and the people of Constantinople rejoiced. After ten years of subjugation, the Persians had been annihilated and the empire of Christ vindicated. When Heraclius entered Constantinople after six years of war he rode in triumph bearing the relic of the Holy Cross in his arms. The first crusade was concluded by one of the most romantic triumphs in history.

In 629 Heraclius set out on a pilgrimage to Jerusalem to deliver the Holy Cross from St Sophia to its rightful place in the Church of the Resurrection. The ceremonial cavalcade attracted the attention of masses of people who flocked to see him wherever he passed – the fluttering pennons of the horsemen with their flashing steel helmets, the casket of the Holy Cross under an embroidered cloth, and in the midst of all, the emperor and his attendants in a blaze of gold and purple.

But all was not well in the Byzantine Empire. When Heraclius reached Emessa (Homs in Syria) a sealed letter was delivered to him by the governor of Bostra. It was a message from Mohammed in Medina inviting him to adopt Islam (for a translation of the letter see the Appendix).[4] Heraclius wrote a courteous reply in which he refused the offer.[5] When he reached Tiberias he was approached by a delegation of Jews who asked for a pledge of security in writing – they feared Christian vengeance in Jerusalem.[6] Heraclius granted it.

When the cavalcade approached the Holy City a great procession of the clergy and monks, carrying gospels, tapers and censers and followed by a multitude of the faithful, came out to greet him. So accompanied, Heraclius approached the Golden Gate on the eastern side of the city[7] where the patriarch Zacharias had come out to meet him. He dismounted, took off his purple cloak and golden breastplate, and in the guise of a humble pilgrim carried the casket with the cross in his arms, following in the footsteps of Zacharias along the Via Dolorosa to the rebuilt Church of the Holy Sepulchre. Everywhere signs of ruin wrought on the city by the Persians were still visible. The emperor praised Modestus, a monk who had assisted in the restoration of the church in Zacharias' absence, and took part in a service of the Exaltation of the Cross, a feast still celebrated by the Eastern and Western Churches on 14 September. Intact in its splendid case, the holy relic was placed on the altar with solemn rites of great magnificence. Sebeos described how all Jerusalem was 'weeping and sobbing and shedding tears, so that that the choir could not sing the songs of the Lord'. Gold coins were minted to commemorate the event.

If this was the climax of the first crusade, what followed was an abysmal let-down. Under pressure from the Christians, Heraclius overlooked his guarantee of safety to the Jews. They were driven out of the city and forbidden to come within 3 miles of its walls. Eutychius and Makrizi claimed that there was a massacre, but this has not been confirmed by other historians.[8] Whatever the truth may be, we know for certain that many Jews fled south into the desert beyond Jordan.

Here they encountered a new phenomenon: the entire area was uniting under the leadership of Mohammed. It was in 622, when Heraclius set off to fight the Persians, that Mohammed fled from Mecca to Medina and ushered in the era of Islam. From Medina he embarked on a career of unrivalled conquest which filled him with great confidence. By 627 he was sending letters to all the kings and religious leaders, asking them to convert to Islam and sealing the letters with his name, Mohammed, the Apostle of God. The letters were delivered to the rulers of Yemen, Oman, Yamamah and Bahrain. There followed messages to Al Harith, the leader of the Saracens, to Cyrus the Mukaukas, the Melkite patriarch of Alexandria,[9] to Chosroes, king of Persia, to Negus of Ethiopia and to Heraclius, emperor of the Romans.[10]

Of the princes of Arabia, the rulers of Yamamah and Bahrain consented immediately and professed their conversion. From Yemen and Oman came curt refusals, which Mohammed received with anger; from the king of Ethiopia a polite, non-committal reply. We do not know who exactly received the letter in Egypt, but according to Arab historians the Egyptians promised to think about the message, treated the envoy with great courtesy and sent him back with numerous gifts, among them two Christian girls, Mary and Shirin, a mule, a donkey and a bag full of money. Later on, Mary adopted Islam and became one of the favourites of Mohammed. The answer of the Persian king Chosroes was to tear up the letter in angry scorn and order the Persian governor of Hamyar, a region bordering Arabia, to send him the severed head of the impudent impostor. 'So shall God rend his kingdom', Mohammed is said to have prophesied when he heard how Chosroes had dealt with his letter.

After the conquest of Mecca the name of Mohammed resounded in the remotest deserts of Arabia. As he set out north from Medina, princes of Arabia began to throw their lot in with him. The following 'Year of Deputations' saw the whole area united under a single man. The fall of Chosroes had broken the Persian dominion of Yemen; like the Egyptians, the Christians of Arabia were predominantly Monophysite and hostile to Constantinople. Everything worked in Mohammed's favour.

In the spring of 632 he made his last pilgrimage to Mecca where he established the ritual still followed by the Muslim faithful. Two months later he sounded the signal for war with the Byzantine Empire. Shortly thereafter he died, but his death only strengthened the cause of Islam. Abu Bakr became caliph, summoned the princes and chiefs of Arabia to give their forces to the Muslim army, and within a year launched an expedition to Syria.

Heraclius did not perceive the growing unity of the Arab tribes in the south as a threat to the empire. Had he confronted the Arabs when everyone was still behind him he might have stopped their advance. Instead, he focused his efforts on unifying the Church. He spent the winter in Jerusalem preoccupied with the work of reorganizing the administration of the eastern provinces that had been thrown out of order by six years of war with Persia. Patriarch Zacharias had died that winter and the emperor appointed Modestus in his place.

When Heraclius left Jerusalem he made for Babylonia through Damascus, Emesa, Borea and Hierapolis (Mambij) to Edessa (Urfa).[11] It was at Hierapolis that he convened a meeting between Athanasius of Antioch, Paul of Armenia and Cyrus of Phasis in the Caucasus. The proclaimed result was complete agreement on the terms of doctrinal compromise, which Heraclius hoped would bring peace to the divided Church. It was followed by the immediate appointment of Cyrus to the primacy of Alexandria with instructions to bring the Melkite and Coptic Churches together. Heraclius had also asked Modestus to help restore the Nestorian Churches to orthodoxy. The following winter Modestus died; failing to find a bishop willing to execute his policies of uniting the Church, Heraclius left the patriarchal throne of Jerusalem vacant.

Initially, the patriarch Athanasius of Antioch, a professed Monophysite, had consented to the compromise demanded by Heraclius at Hierapolis; his formal reinstatement by the emperor depended on it. Whether he subsequently found that he could not persuade his people or simply changed his mind is not clear, but he quickly abandoned the compromise and continued preaching as before. Heraclius retorted by a threat of persecution and appointed Sophronius patriarch of Jerusalem.

It is far from clear why he chose Sophronius, since the latter was openly hostile to the compromise: his first act as patriarch was to call a council at which he denounced the emperor's proposal and anathematized all patriarchs who adopted it. Perhaps Heraclius hoped that Sophronius' appointment would encourage him to have a change of heart. Sophronius may have accepted the post in the belief that Heraclius would have a change of heart. Whatever their reasons, neither of them wavered. This caused tension, and in order to resolve the crisis a delegation was sent from Antioch to Constantinople to plead on behalf of the Syrian Christians. The delegates were received in peevish silence; Heraclius was displeased but said nothing. Barhebreus, himself a Syrian Monophysite, described the occasion with the following words: 'When our people complained to Heraclius he gave no answer. Therefore, the God of vengeance delivered us out of the hands of the Romans by means of the Arabs. Then although our churches were not restored to us, since under Arab rule each Christian community retained its actual possessions, still it profited us not a little to be saved from the cruelty of the Romans and their bitter hatred against us.'[12] The Christians of Syria welcomed the Arabs as deliverers from the rule of their fellow Christians. The emperor's scheme for religious union was simply impossible and it led to his ruin.

Heraclius' treatment of the Jews also came to haunt him. Shortly after he left Edessa the Jews had called a gathering, to which representatives from all the twelve tribes were invited.[13] Together they decided to defy Heraclius and close themselves behind the gates of the city. Heraclius turned back and laid siege to the town, and they capitulated. He granted the Jews easy terms and told them to return peaceably to their towns. But the Jews no longer trusted him. Many fled to the desert and in 634 joined the armies of Islam, acting as guides to the country. And thus, five years after his liberation of Palestine, Heraclius had lost it again. The Arabs, whom he had regarded as just another desert tribe causing trouble on the frontier, had surprised him. So had the Jews and even his fellow Christians. Now Heraclius had to prepare for another war.

The army he sent to Syria to confront the Arabs was under the command of his brother Theodore. The latter had proved an inept general and lost battle after battle, yet he was kept in his post until Heraclius' death. The Arab campaign in Syria unfolded with alarming speed. In September 634 the Byzantine army was defeated, first at Gabatha and then at Yarmouk. After that the Arabs crossed the River Jordan and Bostra fell into their hands; a few days later they laid siege to Damascus. It was here that the Byzantine army caught up with them and fought a desperate battle for the Syrian capital. The result of this confrontation long hung in doubt, but once the Arabs began gaining ground they routed the Byzantine legions.

Heraclius received the news at Antioch. Instead of rushing to the front, he called an assembly in the Cathedral of Antioch. Speech failed him and he asked for council. An old man got up and said: 'The Romans are now suffering for their disobedience to the Gospel, for their quarrels and dissentions, their usury and violence. They must pay a price for their sins.' This was enough for Heraclius; in September 636 he took ship for Constantinople and uttered the often-quoted words: 'Farewell, a long farewell to Syria!'

In Jerusalem, the Christians seized the precious vessels they had received but a few years earlier and sent them aboard ship to the court in Constantinople. The treasures were delivered to Heraclius at his palace near Chalcedon, where he was reported to have stayed for some time in a state of complete derangement.[14] The Holy Cross was returned to St Sophia; in 670 the pilgrim Arculfus had seen it displayed in the cathedral. In the tenth century the emperor and scholar Constantine VII Porphyrogenitus recorded that it was still there, but its subsequent fate is not known.

In Damascus, the prefect Mansur surrendered the city and signed a treaty with the Arabs, which secured the life and property of the inhabitants and allowed them to keep the churches and practise their religion. The Arab army now advanced on Jerusalem and laid siege to the Holy City. The walls and bulwarks of Jerusalem had been strengthened since the Persian occupation; the city was also well provisioned with food. Historians disagree about the length of the siege; it seems to have lasted through the winter of 636-7, possibly longer. But no hope of help came from the Byzantine armies and eventually, under the threat of imminent famine, the patriarch Sophronius agreed to surrender the city. His one demand was that the caliph would come in person to settle the capitulation. Thus it fell to Omar to take Jerusalem. His arrival on a camel has since been described by many historians. His attire was simple and his manner respectful. Once he set seal to the treaty he visited the holy places in the company of Sophronius and showed great respect for them. Nevertheless, the shock of this event soon ended the life of patriarch Sophronius of Jerusalem.

The First Inquisition

In autumn 631 the Melkite patriarch Cyrus landed in Alexandria. The Egyptians called him 'Mukaukas' (the one from the Caucasus) because he had previously served as bishop of Phasis in the Caucasus. Heraclius had bestowed on Cyrus the double appointment of Melkite patriarch and civil governor of Egypt, which gave him authority over the *dux*, the military commander. There had been no precedent for this; Heraclius probably intended to make Cyrus' mission easier to accomplish. Once again he had made a bad choice. Cyrus' former experience had hardly prepared him for the tangle of religious, political and racial prejudices he was to face in Egypt.

Shortly before the arrival of Cyrus, the Coptic patriarch Benjamin fled Alexandria. Heraclius had failed to consult him about the intended union between the Melkite and Coptic Churches, and he interpreted this omission as a declaration of war against the Copts. Before leaving the city Benjamin called an assembly of priests and laymen and delivered an emotional sermon calling on them to hold fast to their faith on penalty of death. He also distributed an encyclical to all his bishops, bidding them flee to the mountains and the deserts and warning them that the wrath of Byzantium was about to descend on them. Then he left Alexandria with two companions under cover of darkness. They walked on foot past Mariut and stayed at the monastery of St Mina.[1] After a short rest they made for the monasteries of Wadi el Natrun, which they found almost deserted. They continued their march all the way across the Delta, past Memphis and the pyramids and on to Upper Egypt until they reached the town of Kush where they took refuge in a small monastery in the desert.

When Cyrus settled in Alexandria he made no attempt to see Benjamin. His very presence scattered the Coptic clergy in terror, but Cyrus took no notice. In October 631 (Jerusalem had not yet fallen) Cyrus invited Patriarch Sophronius to a synod intended to extol the virtues of the Monothelite creed and win over the Melkite and the Coptic communities. To his disappointment Sophronius was no help at all – instead of supporting the creed he opposed it. Cyrus failed to persuade even his own Melkites. To the Melkites the doctrine of the single *will* appeared as the surrender of Chalcedon. To the Copts (those few who were present) it appeared that one *will* meant one *nature* and that in fact Cyrus had come over to the Monophysites. The Copts considered themselves to be the moral winners of the debate, but they still rejected the proposed union. Cyrus lost his nerve: he ended the synod with a resolute proclamation that from now on Monothelism would be the true faith and smote with nine anathemas everyone who rejected it.

The Coptic Church made a mistake in scorning the offer of union; their rejection of compromise cost them untold suffering. After all, there was not much difference between Monophysite and Monothelite. But the Copts had come to believe that changing one iota of their faith would mean betraying the cause of their religious independence, a cause for which they had struggled since the Council of Chalcedon.

At this point Heraclius made one more attempt at union. Sergius had suggested a new compromise: while one *will* should be recognized, the question whether its operation was *single* or *twofold* should be waived and discussion forbidden. Heraclius had secured the support of the Roman Pope Honorius for Sergius' solution (or evasion); he embodied it in a formal edict and distributed it throughout the empire as law. John, the general of the militia, was instructed to take the edict personally to Cyrus along with a cross of special sanctity.[2] But Heraclius' policy misfired; the edict only caused more opposition. Sophronius came out against it while to the Copts it sounded even worse than what was offered before.

We ought to note that the edict might not have reached the Copts beyond Alexandria. Coptic annals of the period reveal no awareness that any compromise had been offered to them at all; Cyrus probably took little trouble to explain the refinements of imperial theology to them. Having acquired despotic power he simply set out the plain alternatives – union or persecution.

The marble streets of Alexandria came to ring with the noise of Byzantine legions. The long line of defensive walls became crowded with soldiers and the mighty towers fitted with engines of war.[3] A month after the failed synod of October 631, the Great Persecution began. Army garrisons were sent throughout the cities of the Delta: Athrib, Nikiu and Babylon. From there they made their way to the Fayoum and the south, all the way to Syene and the First Cataract.

Then Cyrus unleashed his fury. The biography of Isaac, who served as Coptic patriarch from 690 to 693, describes how he met a priest called Joseph who had been hailed before a tribunal of Cyrus. When a confession of his faith was wrung from Joseph, he was beaten with many stripes. Benjamin's own brother Menas was burnt with torches 'till the fat dropped from both his sides to the ground';[4] when he failed to reveal where Benjamin was hiding, his teeth were pulled out and he was put in a sack filled with sand and taken out to sea. Three times he was offered his life if he acknowledged the Council of Chalcedon. Three times he refused and in the end he was drowned. The biographer of Benjamin added: 'It was not they who were victorious over Menas, but Menas, who by Christian patience overcame them.'

Much evidence points to the personal cruelty of Cyrus. The *Life of*

Samuel of Kalamun[5] describes how Samuel, who raised his voice against Cyrus, was captured and brought before him, his hands tied behind his back, an iron collar about his neck and pushed on like a thief. Cyrus questioned him and had him beaten repeatedly 'till his blood ran like water'. In spite of his wounds Samuel called Cyrus 'Son of Satan, Antichrist and Beguiler' to his face. Cyrus ordered his execution, but the prefect of the Fayoum helped Samuel to escape.

The Ethiopian version of the *Life of Abba Samuel* described the arrival of military commander Maximianus at the head of 200 soldiers at Samuel's monastery in the desert. They presented him with a document requiring his subscription to the faith of Chalcedon. Samuel tore it to pieces and flung it out the door of the church saying: 'We have no patriarch but Benjamin! Cursed be the blasphemous document of the Roman emperor; cursed be the Council of Chalcedon and those who believe in it!' Samuel was beaten and left for dead, but recovered and made his way to the monastery of Kalamun.

The Copts in the Delta probably faced the same fate: stripes, torture, imprisonment and death (fig. 29). Melkite bishops were appointed to every city in Egypt up to Ansina;[6] those among the Coptic clergy who survived scattered to various hiding places. Copts who could not flee to the deserts maintained secret observances. In Alexandria a priest called Agathon risked his life to administer secret rites to his Coptic brethren. He later became Benjamin's great friend and successor as patriarch.

The search for Benjamin was unrelenting. Severus claimed that he moved from one fortified convent to another. This seems logical if he was to escape all the search parties looking for him up and down the Nile Valley for ten years. Some authors assigned him a refuge in the White Monastery of Anbba Shenouda, others placed him in the desert near Kush; there were endless caves and rock-cut churches in the mountains near Kush. If he was on the run he may have spent time in all these convents.

It is hardly surprising that Cyrus managed to achieve the conversion of some of the Copts; the entire population could not turn into martyrs. Yet it would be fair to say that by and large the spirit of the Copts was unbroken. We have records that the monastery of al Sukuniya near Matra resisted Cyrus successfully.[7] Some Copts in Mariut even hatched a plot on his life, but a Byzantine officer discovered their secret meetings and sent soldiers to apprehend them. The conspirators were killed, wounded and maimed without any trial.

In the spring of 639 Syria was conquered by the armies of Islam. The conquest of the Holy City of Jerusalem marked the great entry of the Muslims into the Byzantine world. It was the beginning of a war that would end only in 1453 with the fall of Constantinople. From Syrian refugees the Copts in Egypt had heard how Muslims had treated the Syrian Christians; their rule sounded less unbearable than the rule of the most Christian of emperors.

29. Coptic textile showing a Byzantine soldier executing a kneeling prisoner, sixth century. The Pushkin Museum of Fine Arts, Moscow.

7. The First Inquisition

Even after the death of Heraclius, Cyrus 'far from abandoning his rage against the flock of God, or ceasing to persecute it, added violence to violence'.[8] Heraclius' peacemaker in Egypt had become a tyrant and a monster. He had cut the last thread that bound the allegiance of the Copts to the Christian empire and misgoverned Egypt into such hatred of the empire that all hope of peace and reconciliation passed away. When the Egyptians heard of the advance of the Arabs they took the news as a sign of divine vengeance upon their persecutors.

Arabs at the Gates

The ensuing Arab campaign, as described by Arab historians, is of unique interest in elucidating the last years of Byzantine rule in Egypt.[1] It appears that the military commander 'Amr ibn el 'As, who had fought together with Khalid in the decisive battle of Yarmouk, unfolded his plan for the invasion of Egypt to caliph Omar immediately after the surrender of Jerusalem. At the time, Omar was against it; he had just made Khalid governor of Syria and he was unwilling to weaken his forces by detaching an army strong enough to accomplish the task. When 'Amr offered to get a head start with 3,500 cavalry Omar thought that he had underestimated the difficulties and could only promise to think it over.

It may be useful to describe 'Amr in more detail, as his character and personal distinction influenced the course of the Egyptian campaign in ways that could not have been foreseen. At the time of the invasion of Egypt 'Amr was about 45 years old. Though short in stature he was strongly built and excelled in swordsmanship and horsemanship. He was renowned for his eloquence and quickness of wit and described by many as 'the cleverest of the Arabs'.[2] 'When I was with 'Amr,' wrote Umarah, 'I found a man of most intelligent conversation, an excellent companion and councellor.' Ibn Hajar wrote: 'I have never met a man who understood the Quran better, or was more honest and open in his dealings.'

'Amr was of the tribe of the Kuraish and converted to Islam by Mohammed himself. The Prophet's opinion of him was high: he had praised him as the best of the Muslims and most trustworthy of men;[3] it was Mohammed who had raised him to the rank of military commander. 'Amr was renowned for his iron will and unfaltering courage in battle; he inspired absolute trust and personal devotion in his men. He also made them laugh and entertained them with his love of music and verse. 'In 'Amr there mingled something at once of soldier, saint, adventurer and poet,' wrote Butler.[4] This was the man who conquered Egypt with 3,500 horsemen.

After the Arab conquest of Jerusalem Omar remained in the city and sent 'Amr and his cavalry to lend support to the siege of Caesarea, where Constantine, the son of Heraclius, was in command. But only a few days later 'Amr received a letter from him: Omar had decided to sanction 'Amr's plan for the invasion of Egypt, but ordered 'Amr to keep it secret. 'Amr accordingly departed by dead of night and marched his little army without incident towards the border of Egypt. He had already reached Ra'fa when a messenger in hot haste rode into his camp bearing dispatches from the caliph.

'Amr shrewdly guessed their content: Omar's hesitation had prevailed and he had changed his mind. But 'Amr was not a man to turn back. It occurred to him that if the letter were to find him already in Egypt Omar would have no choice but to pray for his success and send reinforcements. So he refused to receive the letter until he crossed the river-bed (which may have marked the border) and entered the valley of A'rish. He had reached the Great Wall of Egypt, which ran across Kulzum towards the east bank of the Nile. Originally built by Senwosret III and Amenemhat III, mighty pharaohs of ancient Egypt, it had long fallen down and offered no hindrance to the movement of an army; the Arabs called it 'Wall of the Old Woman'. Here, 'Amr read the letter and asked: 'Is this place in Syria or in Egypt?' The answer was: 'In Egypt.' Then he read Omar's dispatch and said: 'The army will advance in accordance with the caliph's order.'

It was on 12 December 639 that 'Amr's little force celebrated the Muslim Day of Sacrifice. The rite was full of solemnity for the desert warriors who were setting out, bound by ties of clanship and devotion, to conquer the land of the pharaohs. They had made their vows and there was no turning back. From the valley of A'rish with its palm groves the road led away from the coast through the waste of desert, relieved by occasional wells and villages. It was the immemorial high road to Egypt that had witnessed the passage of Abraham, Jacob, Joseph and the holy family, the road of caravans, merchants, travellers and pilgrims.

A few miles before Pelusium the road turned north-west, plunging among dunes and moving sand hills. The Arabs made ready to defend themselves against attack, but to their surprise, they encountered no one until they came well within sight of the city. The first Byzantine soldiers they saw were behind the walls of Pelusium. Egypt's border had gone undefended.

Pelusium, the Coptic Peramoun and the Arabic al Farama, stood at the place where an arm of the Nile joined the sea. The city possessed a harbour and a fortress; it was the eastern key to Egypt, commanding the desert approaches, the sea and the waterway to the Delta. The Arab force was too small to lay siege to Pelusium and the only alternative was frequent sallies. Sporadic fighting lasted a month[5] until one of the gates was seized in the repulse of a sally – 'Amr, who led the party, used the chance and quickly entered the city. The Byzantine soldiers fled and he found himself master of Pelusium. He immediately decided to burn the ships and dismantle the fortress. He could spare no troops to hold Pelusium and he judged it better to make it useless to the enemy if recaptured. His line of communication and retreat in case of disaster was now secure. It had also become clear to him that without reinforcements he and his men were doomed to failure: they had at last realized that the task that lay before them was gigantic.

What the Byzantines were thinking is difficult to imagine. Common prudence would have established posts of observation in the desert to give timely warning for the defence of Pelusium. But it seems that the rule of Cyrus had not only demoralized the country, it had made it helpless. Historians have speculated that Cyrus may have planned to forge an alliance with the Arabs against the empire; they were baffled by the fact that the Byzantines did nothing. The loss of Pelusium was the first great Byzantine blunder in the war.

By the middle of January 640 no reinforcements had arrived for 'Amr. Refusing to turn back or wait any longer, he decided to march on. His losses in the fight for Pelusium were made good by a number of Beduin who flocked to his side.[6] After ten years of brutal persecution of the Egyptians there was no love lost between the Byzantines and the people of the desert. From Pelusium 'Amr marched south-west to Migdol, modern Kantir on the Suez Canal. Most ancient conquerors of Egypt, like Cambyses, took a different route, striking due west to Tanis, and from there through the Delta to Bubastis. But by this time the swamps around Lake Manzala had spread and made the route more difficult. 'Amr's army was mounted and had no means of bridging canals and rivers. Moving due south 'Amr crossed the hills.[7] Once he was clear of the *wadi* a short and easy march remained to Bilbais.

Only here did the Byzantines show themselves. During the night the general Aretion, who had fled from Jerusalem, surprised the Arab camp with a fierce onslaught. The Arabs leapt up and set the soldiers to flight. Now they were but one day's ride from the capital of the Delta.

The next day 'Amr and his horsemen rode by Heliopolis, skirted the cultivated land and aimed for a point on the Nile called Umm Dunayn ('the mother of worlds', in what is now the heart of Cairo). Riding up to the Mukkatam hills they looked over the silent lushness of the Egyptian Delta that now stretched before them. Here at last was the fabled Land of Plenty, the food basket of the pharaohs. The little black triangles of the pyramids rose out of the mist over the river, as they had done every day for 3,000 years. The landscape seemed a place of isolated peace, living its own life seemingly unaware of war and invaders. As far as the eye could see black earth put out crops so green, their foliage was like green light. It was the most beautiful landscape the desert warriors had seen. They were surprised and elated by the ease of their approach. Egypt appeared as a country just waiting to be ruled by righteous men.

Only now did Cyrus hasten from Alexandria to Babylon to help assemble the Byzantine troops. Umm Dunayn itself was strongly held and the main force of the Byzantines, secure behind the massive walls of the fortress of Babylon, could choose their own moment when to strike. Several weeks passed in a series of indecisive engagements, which hurt the Byzantines little, but wore down the number of the Arabs, already perilously weak. 'Amr found himself in a serious predicament. He had ridden all over the countryside around him, finding that he could not storm the fortress of Babylon nor seize the city of Misr which adjoined it. The recent battles had weakened his forces. Omar had promised reinforcements and 'Amr sent urgent dispatches to press for their arrival. But there was no sign of their coming. Every day's delay was a gain to the enemy and victory hung in the balance.[8]

It was not in the nature of 'Amr to despair or think of retreat. Recognizing that the capture of Babylon was for the moment out of reach, he decided on a bold diversion – he made a dash for the Fayoum Oasis, a rich province some 50 miles south, on the opposite bank of the Nile. Before leaving he resolved to capture Umm Dunayn at all costs. Arab sources claimed that he assembled his men and began speaking sternly to them, when a trooper murmured: 'We are not made of iron!' 'Silence, you dog!' roared 'Amr. 'If I am a dog,' the man replied, 'you are a leader of dogs,' at which everyone laughed. 'Then let us fight like dogs,' urged 'Amr. They took Umm Dunayn in a wild frenzy and seized enough boats to transport the diminished army across the Nile.

When they had crossed the Nile they marched south to the cultivated land of Memphis. This ancient capital of Egypt had been slowly decaying since the foundation of Alexandria; the town of Misr, which lay on the opposite bank of the Nile, had become far more populous and had even usurped the name of Memphis.

The sight of the mighty ruins and several more pyramids in the distance made a powerful impression on the Arabs. From the pyramids, they crossed the desert to the Fayoum Oasis. The city of Piom or Fayoum was held by governor Domitian and the defence of the province was entrusted to John, a general of the militia who had been appointed by emperor Heraclius himself. The points of entrance to the Fayoum were strongly guarded; promptly, a force of cavalry and archers was sent to stop the Arab march.

Finding it impossible to break through the Byzantine cordon, the Arabs took to the desert hills, capturing a large number of cattle along the way. They advanced to a town called Bahnasa, which they took by storm, slaughtering all before them – men, women, children.[9]

Suddenly, they had to turn around – a small force of fifty Byzantines was on their tail. 'Amr and his bodyguard galloped towards them at full speed and forced them to retreat. The Arabs were choosing scouts to follow the Byzantines to their camp when a Bedouin chief appeared and volunteered to lead them to it by another road, hidden by high sand dunes. They followed him to the camp, swiftly surrounded it and killed everyone to the last man. This was how John, the friend of Heraclius, perished.

'Amr had accomplished more than he expected. Though he had failed to capture the city of Fayoum, he had extricated his army from a dangerous position at Umm Dunayn and removed it to a place of comparative safety. He had also killed the governor of the Fayoum. Above all he had gained time. The long-delayed reinforcements were beginning to arrive and he retraced his steps north in order to meet them.

On 6 June the army sent by Omar arrived in the neighbourhood of Heliopolis. No one stopped them. The men were under the command of al Zubair, a kinsman and companion of the Prophet Mohammed. The legion numbered 4,000 men, but at a short distance two columns of equal strength followed them, so that the total reinforcements amounted to 12,000.

The Byzantine army could easily have faced 'Amr while he was still isolated, but they did nothing. No one prevented the horsemen from crossing the river and meeting their reinforcements. Once again Theodore lost his opportunity and 'Amr's men, elated with their adventures, rode into the Muslim camp at Heliopolis cheered by their fellow Arabs. Everyone felt that victory for Islam hung in the air.

9

The Fall of Babylon

At Babylon general Theodore[1] had been drawing troops from the towns of the Delta; by the time he had amassed an army capable of driving the Arabs out of Heliopolis, all the reinforcements sent by Omar had arrived, and 'Amr found himself at the head of 15,000 men. They included some of the most renowned soldiers of Islam. According to Abu'l Mahasin,[2] the following companions of the Prophet were part of the army: 'Amr and his son Abdallah, Zubair, Abdallah, son of caliph Omar, Sa'ad Abu Wakkas (whose presence is disputed), Kharija ibn Hudafah, Khais as Sahmi, Mikdad ibn al Aswad, Abdallah ibn Abu Sarh, Nafi al Fahri, Abu Rafi', freedman of the Apostle of God, Ibn Hasanah, two sons of Shurabil and Wardan, the freedman of 'Amr. Abu'l Mahasin emphasized the reputation these fighters enjoyed – they had to prove victorious or die to the last man. What numbers the Byzantines mustered can only be conjectured, but most ancient historians agree that they had superiority and that the soldiers in the Byzantine army could not have numbered any fewer than 20,000. It is not entirely clear how many were within the walls of Babylon and in the camp at Heliopolis on this occasion.

'Amr's plan was to draw the Byzantine army away from Babylon onto the open plain. Alhough the Byzantines had some cavalry, the bulk of the army was foot soldiers, spearmen and archers. When 'Amr's spies had given him warning of their movement, he detached under cover of night two bodies of troops, one not far from Umm Dunayn and the other in the fold of the Mukkatam hills, close to what is now the Citadel of Cairo. The line of Byzantine advance thus lay between two detached corps of fighters who had orders to fall on the flank and rear of the enemy.

Early in the morning the Byzantine forces emerged from the gardens and monasteries of Heliopolis and deployed in the open. They stood ready to meet 'Amr's cavalry head on. The clash between the two armies took place about half way between the two camps, somewhere in the region of modern Abbasiya. It was a desperate fight. When the battle was at its fiercest, the Arab detachment under Kharija issued from the hills and fell like a whirlwind on the tail of the Byzantines. Caught between two forces the Byzantines fell into disorder and moving towards Umm Dunayn were attacked by a further Arab contingent. Disorder now turned into disaster. Foot soldiers pressed towards the river and seized boats to sail back to Babylon; a great many were cut down and drowned. Of the Byzantine garrison all but 300 perished in the fight.

When the soldiers in Babylon heard the news, they lost heart and fled down the river by boat to Nikiu. The town of Misr, which had been protected by the fort of Babylon, was now at the mercy of the Arabs. It was captured without further fighting. Moving their camp up from Heliopolis, the Arabs pitched it north and east of the fortress of Babylon, in the region known to subsequent generations as Fustat.

News of the Arab victory caused the new Byzantine governor of the Fayoum, Domitian, to evacuate the city by night and flee to the safety of the monastery of Nikiu without telling his people. As soon as this was reported to 'Amr, he flung a body of troops across the Nile and captured the capital amid scenes of ruthless massacre; the whole province was now brought under Muslim control.

Panic spread through the Delta. The people, who had suffered for 20 years at the hands of the Persians and the Byzantines, despaired. Men, women and children streamed towards Alexandria, abandoning land and houses, goods, cattle and crops. They were happy that the Nile was rising and making the Delta impassable.

By the beginning of September, at the height of the flood, 'Amr had no choice but to remain near Babylon. He now decided to lay siege to the city. The massive walls and lofty towers of the fortress encircled by the Nile – and the moat was now full of water – promised a long resistance to the Arabs who had no siege equipment and knew nothing of engineering. Some engines of war had been captured in the Fayoum and in Trajan's citadel at Manuf, but the Arabs had no skill to operate them or to keep them in repair.[3] Opposite the fortress lay the island of Roda; at times of peace it was connected to the fortress by a line of boats. Though the Byzantines had dismantled the bridge, pontoons were left moored by the gate of the fortress and boats passed readily from the gate to the island. 'Amr was unable to master the river; its swelling tide had baffled far more skilful navigators. He was afraid that if he began an attack from the river, his boats might be swept away by currents or sunk by catapults from the fortress.

Patriarch Cyrus was within the walls of Babylon. Theodore had fled to Alexandria after the defeat in Heliopolis, and nominally Cyrus was in command.[4] The soldiers could have amounted to no more than 5,000 or 6,000 men, but the garrison was amply provided with food and other equipment. The civil population had been swollen by a number of refugees from the adjacent city of Misr, but Cyrus sent many away by river. The churches were Melkite; Copts were not tolerated.[5]

At the beginning of October 640 Cyrus summoned the Melkite bishop of Babylon to a secret council of war: he proposed that they offer a sum of money to the enemy and buy them off to leave Egypt. The Melkite bishop agreed. They decided to keep the plan secret from the army and in the middle of the night they opened the gate of Babylon. Cyrus and a few trusted men quietly descended to the river, cast off the boats and rowed to the isle of Roda, from where they sent envoys to the Arab camp on the other side. They took the precaution of removing the pontoon boats from Roda to prevent any soldiers from landing at Roda should they notice Cyrus' absence and decide to follow.

'Amr courteously received the envoys of Cyrus in the Arab camp. He gave no immediate answer to Cyrus' proposal. Instead, he kept the envoys in the camp for two days and allowed them to go about freely.

The simplicity and enthusiasm of the Arabs deeply impressed the Melkites. They later reported to Cyrus: 'We have seen a people who prefer death to life and humility to pride. They sit in the dust and they take their meals on horseback. Their commander is one of themselves, there is no distinction of rank among them. They have fixed hours of prayer, at which they all pray, first washing their hands and feet, and they pray with reverence.'[6]

After two days 'Amr gave his answer. It was short and clear: 'Only one of three courses is open to you: (1) Islam with brotherhood and equality; (2) payment of tribute and protection with an inferior status; (3) war till God decides between us.'

Cyrus was happy to see his envoys return. When he heard 'Amr's terms, he reasoned that it was better to reach an agreement now, while the Arab forces were hemmed in by the floods. He asked 'Amr to send special envoys to the fortress of Babylon to discuss the terms of agreement in front of the others. He returned to the fortress, unobserved by the soldiers.

'Amr sent ten of his officers headed by a trusted friend, Ubayda ibn as-Samit. The Arabs were ferried across to the island of Roda and from Roda to Babylon. Ubayda was ushered into the presence of Cyrus who was seated flanked by army officers. At the sight of Ubayda Cyrus leapt up from his seat – he was shocked to see that Ubayda was black. The Arabs laughed; they explained that Ubayda was one of their most trusted and capable leaders and that 'Amr had appointed him personally to negotiate the truce. They said that the Muslims held black and white men in equal respect and that there were thousands of black men among their companions. They all lived to fight for God and follow his will. They did not care about wealth as long as they could satisfy their hunger and clothe their bodies. This world was nothing to them; the next world was all.

Cyrus replied: 'I have listened to your account of yourself and your comrades and I understand why your arms have prevailed.' Then he proposed something entirely different: the payment of two *denarii* a head for every man in the Arab army, 100 *denarii* for their commander and 1,000 to their caliph, on condition that they return to their own country. Ubayda refused. When Cyrus persisted, Ubayda threw his hands up in the air: 'No! By the Lord of heaven and earth and all things, you shall have no other terms from us. So make your choice!'

Cyrus and his companions held a consultation. They returned to face Ubayda, saying they had ruled out conversion to Islam, a religion they knew nothing about, but they feared submission would be tantamount to slavery. Ubayda reassured them their persons and property would be respected and the churches and the practice of their religion left un-harmed. The terms thus interpreted appeared reasonable and even generous to Cyrus. He asked for a month to consider the matter. Ubayda gave him three days.

When the soldiers discovered about the secret negotiations of Cyrus they refused to surrender. Three days expired and no answer was sent to 'Amr. On the fourth day, when the armistice was over, the Byzantines sallied over the drawbridge and fell upon the Arab camp. The Arabs, though completely surprised, flew to arms. A battle followed; the Byzan-tines were driven back and after severe losses retreated behind the walls.

After this the soldiers consented to accept 'Amr's terms of subjection and tribute. This arrangement was embodied in a treaty, which was concluded on the express condition that it was subject to the approval of the emperor. Pending ratification, there should be no change in the military situation. The fortress was not surrendered and Cyrus took his leave of Babylon and hastened to Alexandria. From there he sent urgent dispatches to emperor Heraclius in Constantinople.

Heraclius was puzzled. Did the proposed treaty relate to Babylon alone, or did it cover the surrender of all Egypt, including Alexandria? Were the Arabs merely to receive a tribute of money and retire, or were they to remain masters of the country? Was Egypt to be torn away from the empire and delivered to the Muslims?

It was about the middle of November when Cyrus received a peremptory message of recall. His conscience may have quailed as he prepared to meet the emperor. He knew how far he had betrayed the emperor's instructions during ten years of persecution; he could not disguise the fact that his religious mission was a failure and that the ruin of his schemes was bringing about the political ruin of Egypt. Furthermore, his willingness to pay tribute to the enemy clouded his conduct with the suspicion of treach-ery. These thoughts must have weighed heavily on his mind when he approached the emperor's presence in Constantinople.

He met with an angry reception. The emperor asked that he explain himself. Cyrus admitted that he had agreed to pay the gold of Egypt to the Arabs, but he proposed that the tribute might be met by imposing a special tax on merchandise in Alexandria, so that the imperial revenues would not be diminished. As for the rest, he saw no hope. The Arabs were not like other men: they had no earthly wants and would fight to death. If the emperor had met them and seen their fighting powers he would have been forced to acknowledge that they were invincible. It was therefore better to come to terms with them.[7]

Heraclius was furious; he leapt up, called Cyrus an abject coward and a heathen and accused him of betraying the empire. He commanded his arrest and delivered him over to the city prefect at whose hands Cyrus suffered great indignities. In the end he sent him into exile.

The rejection of the treaty by the Byzantine emperor became known to the Arabs by the end of the year 640. All truces or half measures were now over and both sides braced themselves for a fresh struggle. The Nile was falling fast and as its waters were sinking lower and lower, with them sank the courage of the defenders of Babylon. The moat was being emptied and the soldiers spiked the ditch with caltrops, sown more thickly before the gates. Meanwhile, the Arabs began levelling an approach.

By now both sides had somehow become used to each other. Makrizi described an incident when one day a small Byzantine patrol went out of the fortress and fell upon Zubair and Ubayda at the time of their prayers. The Arab chiefs at once leapt on their horses, charged and chased the Byzantines who, as the enemy was gaining upon them, threw off their breastplates and ornaments. When Zubair and Ubayda chased them to the walls of the fortress, Ubayda was suddenly wounded by a stone slung from the battlements. He wiped off the blood, got on his horse and the two friends returned to their place and resumed their prayers, while the Byzantine soldiers came out again and recovered what they had thrown away.

As the winter waned, sallies and combats outside the walls grew more rare. Then news reached 'Amr that Theodore was assembling an army in the country between the two branches of the Nile. 'Amr had no intention of being attacked; leaving a strong enough force to maintain the siege of Babylon, he moved up the Damietta branch of the Nile, crossed the river at Athrib and stuck northwards in the direction of Samanud. Theodore had dispatched two of his generals to hold Samanud and at a junction their column met with a body of the local militia. The latter refused either to fight the Arabs or follow the Byzantine standards, but simply turned around and rode away. But during the ensuing battle of Samanud, the Arabs suffered heavy losses and 'Amr discovered that he could not inflict serious damage on the northern towns, which were protected against cavalry by moats and canals. He therefore retreated to Busir and fortified it; he also fortified Manuf and Athrib and left garrisons within the walls.

But if Theodore won some advantage, he was unable to follow it. And he never succeeded in sending a relieving force anywhere near the beleaguered Babylon. The inaction of Theodore may have been due to heavy desertion on the Byzantine side. The ten-year persecution of the Copts had not only alienated the Egyptians, it had also demoralized the army. In the climate of unashamed self-interest and cruelty, bonds of religion and patriotism had become weak. In Babylon, without any signs of reinforcements, spirits dwindled. The legions tarried.

In March 641 a shout went up in the Muslim camp at the news of the death of Heraclius. 'Amr waited for another month; he did not storm Babylon. After a month had expired his kinsman Zubair lost patience and decided to organize a storming party himself. He filled the moat at a place destined for attack. The assault itself was carried with such swiftness during the night that Zubair's scaling ladder was set against the walls unnoticed. The Arab warrior sprang from it with sword in hand shouting 'Allahu Akbar!'[8]

As the defenders of Babylon rallied, a fierce shower of arrows swept the walls from the outside and gave Zubair's men time to climb up the ladder and jump inside the parapet. Here, the Byzantines, expecting an assault, had blocked the ramparts by a cross wall at either end, so that the scaling party, after overpowering the guard and climbing on top of the wall, found their passage barred. They could go no further; they were unable to reach the stairs that led to the fortress.

Now the defenders had an opportunity, but they surrendered. After a hurried consultation a parley was held and the commander of the fortress offered to capitulate, provided the lives of the soldiers were spared. 'Amr at once approved the terms. A treaty of surrender was drawn up, under which it was agreed that in three days the garrison should evacuate the fortress, retiring by river and carrying only what was necessary for a few days subsistence. An apocryphal story about the fall of Babylon claimed that Ubayda was offended by 'Amr's treaty of surrender: 'If you had only waited a minute longer we would have taken the fort!'

The official arrival of the Arabs took place on Good Friday, 6 April 641. In the interval a fleet of boats was collected from Roda and all preparations made for the retreat of the garrison down the Nile. Two days later, they were leaving. It may have been a sad coincidence for the Christian army that their last day in the fortress coincided with the day of the Resurrection. But neither Easter Day nor the solemnity of their defeat could abate the fury of religious hatred among the defeated. Their last act was to bring up some unfortunate Coptic prisoners from the dungeons of Babylon and mutilate them. John of Nikiu described the moans and tears of the mutilated captives as they were driven out of the fort in scorn. He believed that the fall of Babylon was divine punishment for the Byzantine mistreatment of the Copts. Implacable hatred divided the Melkites and the Copts even at the moment when the fruits of their disunion became visible in the triumph of Islam.

Alexandria Won

'Amr was delighted to have secured the withdrawal of the Byzantines from Babylon. They had neither accepted Islam nor agreed to pay tribute. But in terms of morale, the power of Byzantium was shaken and that of the Arabs greatly strengthened. Tax was imposed on those who stayed behind and many Egyptians chose to convert rather than pay. Aside from the question of money, the offer of equality with the conquerors was probably seen as a mark of honour by the conquered. No other conquerors had ever offered the Egyptians equality. The Romans had discriminated against them regardless of their faith; the Melkite Church had oppressed them for centuries and persecuted them violently for ten years. Now, if they but accepted the Prophet of Arabia as their own, they were taken into the family. The Arabs saw themselves as of the same race, they were far simpler in manner and habit. They prayed together side by side and looked upon all Muslims as brothers.

Though the treaty of Babylon was local, its results were felt all over the Byzantine Empire. Babylon was the gate between Upper and Lower Egypt and anyone planted within the walls of its impregnable fortress not only dominated the Delta, but had Upper Egypt at its mercy. The conquest of Egypt was half accomplished.

'Amr had the pontoon bridges from Babylon to Roda and from Roda to Giza rebuilt, thus spanning the whole width of the Nile and establishing control over river traffic. In less than three months the Nile would begin to rise again, and time was precious. He became anxious to launch his army – it had been confined for months to the camp at Fustat. Dispatches were sent to Omar reporting progress and requesting more troops, and arrangements made for the administration of the conquered town and territory. The walls of Babylon were repaired and a strong garrison left behind with Kharija in command. Then, with his army remounted, 'Amr pushed northwards following the western branch of the Nile. His own tent at Fustat was left in position: he had discovered that a dove had nested at the top and laid her eggs. According to Yakut, 'Amr said: 'She has taken refuge under our protection. Let the tent stand till she has hatched her young and they have all flown away.' A sentinel was left to prevent the dove from being molested.

Having learned his lesson on the previous misadventures in the Delta, 'Amr marched his army on the western (desert) side of the Nile, where his cavalry could move with more freedom, unhampered by the network of canals. The first point on his march was Nikiu, a site on the east side of the Rosetta branch of the Nile.[1] It was not only a flourishing town and a seat of one of the main bishoprics, but also a place of the highest strategic value in the defence of the military route between Babylon and Alexandria.

The first encounter of the Arabs with the Byzantines took place at Tarnut on the Nile, or Tarrana as the Arabs called it, the main point of departure for the Coptic monasteries of Wadi el Natrun. The Byzantines suffered defeat and withdrew, and the Arabs had to cross the river in order to continue their advance on Nikiu. Here, the Byzantines had the opportunity to attack, but Theodore had left the cowardly Domitian in command, the same governor who had fled in panic from the Fayoum. Domitian had a fleet of boats, which he meant to employ for the defence of the town and for attacking the Arabs on their way back across the river. But once again his courage failed him and he fled by boat to Alexandria, abandoning the garrison. Finding themselves betrayed by their leader, the soldiers flung aside their arms and rushed to the canal in an attempt to seize the boats. But panic had also spread among the boatmen – they quickly cast off the boats from their moorings and fled in disorder. The Arabs rode up and fell on the defenceless soldiers in the water, putting everyone to the sword.

The entry of the Arabs into town was unopposed, but they killed and plundered as they advanced. As Nikiu was a stronghold of the Coptic faith, division and disorder began spreading through the country and it was not long before civil war was added to the calamities of Egypt. The Delta was now split in two camps: one part sided with the Byzantines while the other joined the Arabs. Battle, pillage and the burning of towns became common incidents.

The way for the advance on Alexandria was now open. Steadily pushing the enemy before him 'Amr marched north-east, still following the canal which bordered the desert. He found the Byzantine army barring his passage at a place called Suntais, 6 miles south of Damanhur, but this engagement too resulted in the retreat of the Byzantines. They made no effort to rally to Damanhur to hold the town, but streaming north from the battlefield, they struck the high road to Alexandria, crossed the nearly empty canal and after a march of some 20 miles took refuge in the fort of Kariun. It was the last of the fortresses between Babylon and Alexandria, controlling the canal on which the city depended for food and water.

Here, Theodore resolved to make his last stand. The Byzantine army put up a remarkable fight. The countryside around Alexandria had flocked to Theodore's side and the fighting was severe, lasting for ten days. In the drawn-out battle 'Amr's son Abdallah was badly wounded and 'Amr prayed 'the prayer of fear'. At the end of ten days the Arabs were victorious, capturing the fortress of Kariun and driving back the Byzantine army. Theodore now retreated behind the gates of Alexandria.[2]

10. Alexandria Won

The capture of Kariun had completely cleared the way to the capital, and as soon as the troops had recovered from the strain of recent fighting, 'Amr moved on. He didn't stop until they came within sight of Alexandria. Standing on the desert ridge that overlooked the sea, the Arabs were mesmerized by the sight. The soldiers had seen Edessa, Damascus and Jerusalem, but nothing had prepared them for the magnificence of the city which now rose before them. As far as the eye could see there was a long line of walls and towers; domes and pediments gleamed before them, columns, obelisks, colossal statues, temples and palaces. The Serapeum shone on the hill with its golden roof and the Cathedral of St Mark opposite, on the shore. Out to sea towered the lighthouse of Pharos, one of the Wonders of the World. The Arabs were moved by the stateliness and grandeur of the city they had come to conquer.

They also realized they did not possess a single vessel or engine of war. On the north the city was defended by the sea; on the south by a canal and Lake Mariut, on the west by the Gate of the Sun. Alexandria's walls were armed with powerful artillery; the Byzantines had every reason to be confident. When 'Amr launched his troops in a mad tilt against the walls, the catapults on the battlements hurled such a rain of heavy stones against them that they were driven back out of range. All they could do was pitch camp at a respectful distance in the hope that the enemy might be unwise enough to sally out and give battle.

'Amr knew that the flood season was approaching again and he felt that his best tactic was to make his presence felt elsewhere. He marched back to Kariun and Damanhur and struck eastward 22 miles north of modern Tanta. Once again he found strong walls encompassed by water and once again he and his army had to retreat. They pushed southwards, following the canal known as Bahr el Nuzam until they came to Tukh and Damsis. At both places they were easily repulsed. The only thing they could do was burn the crops ripening for the harvest. No other progress could be made. 'Amr returned to Babylon.

In the meantime, great changes had taken place in Constantinople. After the death of Heraclius on 11 February 641, power was divided between his two sons, Constantine and Heraclius II (also called Heraclonas). This was an impossible compromise. The strong-willed second wife of Heraclius and mother of Heraclonas, Martina, had virtually ruled at the end of her husband's life. She was not a woman to accept the division of authority easily. Her own designs in favour of her son met with strong resistance. The successor of Patriarch Sergius, Pyrrhus, sided against Martina with Constantine and proclaimed him emperor to the exclusion of Martina and her children. In response, Martina had Pyrrhus kidnapped and secretly conveyed to an island west of Africa.[3]

Sebeos wrote that before Heraclius died, he had made Constantine swear to show mercy on all prisoners and to recall all whom he had banished. This may be why Constantine sent a fleet to bring the disgraced

Cyrus back from exile. Martina had also pressed for his recall because she was sure of his sympathy with her ambitions. We do not know where Cyrus was exiled nor how long it took him to return to Constantinople. But in the interim Theodore was also summoned from Egypt. Theodore was not in favour of peace and prevailed on the emperor to send large reinforcements to fight the Arabs. But Constantine was seized by an illness and died on 25 May 641 after a reign of about 100 days.[4] Martina profited from his death and proclaimed her son emperor; the renewed ascendancy of Martina kindled resentment, which soon flamed into rebellion. In the aftermath, Constans II was crowned in association with Heraclonas.

The latter had already arranged for the restoration of Cyrus to his seat in Alexandria. Cyrus was sent to Egypt, authorized by the emperor to conclude peace with the Arabs. Cyrus may have impressed on the emperor his conviction of the necessity of surrender. Martina too favoured peace with the Arabs at any price. What tangle of motives lay behind this policy is uncertain. But Theodore's plan for resistance had failed and he found himself accompanying Cyrus on his arrival in the Royal Harbour of Alexandria on the morning of the Day of the Holy Cross, 14 September 641.

Men, women and children, young and old, had flocked to the Royal Harbour for the arrival of Cyrus. He was carrying on his person a cross of special sanctity, which was said to enclose a portion of the Holy Cross itself.[5] The treasured relic was carried by Cyrus in procession to the Caesareum. It was an occasion of great solemnity: banners of silk fluttered, smoke of incense rose and hymns were sung. The streets were thronged with people treading upon one another; hearts leaped and eyes blinked with the dazzle of brilliant colours and golden crosses, and the patriarch had the utmost difficulty in making his way through the excited crowds.

In robes of white brocade, wearing a large golden dome on his head, Cyrus held himself with dignity and moved slowly forward. His white beard was parted from chin to waist, so that all might see the display of gold and gems that covered his chest. The priests behind him were in cloth of gold, brand new and gleaming. After the priests came the choir-boys, mouths opening and shutting, their voices lost in the general din.

Arriving at the cathedral, Cyrus shook hands with the military commander and distinguished guests and mounted the steps to the door. He was visibly shaken by the ordeal. Nevertheless, he turned around, raised his arms in blessing and attempted a benign smile at the crowds. Inside, a festival service was held in honour of the relic and a sermon delivered by the younger deacons on the Exaltation of the Cross.[6] Unfortunately, the service ended unhappily. One of the deacons had recited an improper psalm, which went against the canon. The people interpreted this as an evil omen. They found Cyrus looking very ill; his exile had physically worn him down and the exertion of his rough passage through the crowds had tried his strength. Many wondered whether he would look upon another Easter.

Towards the end of October Cyrus made his way to Babylon where 'Amr had just returned; he had been waging war in the towns of the Delta and in Upper Egypt. We are told that a small column of the Arabs had got as far as Ansina, the capital of the Thebaid. Byzantine troops had not yet withdrawn from this region and some commanders wondered if they should offer resistance to the Arabs. But the governor of Ansina, John, had refused to fight; he had no wish to meet the fate of the Fayoum garrison. He seized all the public money and carried it with his troops, making his way across the desert to Alexandria. In the Fayoum, which was already settling to Arab rule as a tributary province, sentiments had gone so far that the people killed any Byzantine soldier they chanced to meet. Further south the Copts had even less incentive to fight for the empire.

'Amr received Cyrus in the fortress of Babylon. This time, he was the master. He remarked with great confidence: 'You have done well to come to us.' The patriarch said that in order to put an end to the war, the people would be willing to pay tribute, adding: 'God had given this country to you. Let there be no more enmity between you and the Byzantines.' An arrangement was reached and a treaty signed on 8 November 641.

The terms of this treaty were variously reported by the Arab sources;[7] John of Nikiu cited the agreements as follows:

1. Payment of a fixed tribute by all who came under the treaty.
2. Armistice of eleven months, to expire on the first day of the Coptic month of Paophi, i.e. 28 September 642.
3. During the armistice the Arab forces could maintain their position, but they should keep away and undertake no military operations against Alexandria; the Byzantine forces were to cease all acts of hostility.
4. The garrison at Alexandria could depart by sea, carrying all their possessions and treasures with them; any Byzantine soldiers leaving Egypt by land were to pay a monthly tribute on their journey.
5. No Byzantine army was to return or attempt the recovery of Egypt.
6. The Muslims were to respect Christian churches and not interfere in any way with Christian practices.
7. The Jews were to remain in Alexandria.
8. 150 military and 50 civilian hostages were to be given by the Byzantines until the due execution of the treaty.[8]

The payment of tribute and taxes by the Copts (*akhl al dhimmah*) implied they had a privileged status of a protected people. The tribute was fixed at two *denarii* per head for all except the very old and children; in addition to the capitation tax, a land tax or property tax was imposed. The number of the able-bodied male population was variously given by the Arab authorities, but the total capitation tax was generally estimated to amount to 12,000,000 *denarii*. John of Nikiu's version of the treaty said nothing about the date of the first payment of tribute, but Ibn Khaldun noted that it was expected as soon as the agreement was signed 'and the overflow of the river had ceased'.

When the treaty was signed, 'Amr called Mu'awiya al Kindi and told him to take the news of the surrender to caliph Omar. Mu'awiya asked for a letter, but 'Amr said contemptuously: 'What do I have to do with a letter? Are you not an Arab who can give a report of what you have witnessed?'

For his part, Cyrus hastened to Alexandria, bearing the treaty with him. He presented it to Theodore, whose acquiescence is somewhat puzzling, considering that he advocated military resistance. Perhaps he realized that no other option was open to him during the rule of Heraclonas. Dispatches were sent to Heraclonas, announcing the terms of surrender and recommending them for ratification. The population of Alexandria was kept in the dark; news of the treaty was exchanged in confidential whispers among the commanders.

The Alexandrians discovered what was going on only when they saw an Arab force suddenly advancing towards the city. Alarms rang out and from every corner men and women ran towards the defensive walls and the towers. From there they could see the Arabs riding forward unconcerned; meanwhile Byzantine generals tried to calm them down, arguing that further resistance was impossible and hopeless. When the Arabs came within range of the Byzantine artillery they put up the flags of truce. Answering signals were made; a few horsemen rode within speaking distance. They shouted that they had not come to attack but to collect the tribute promised them by Cyrus.

As news of this spread throughout the city, the furious and incredulous crowd tore through the streets towards the palace. When Cyrus appeared on the steps, the people ran towards him ready to stone him. Stopping their rage with a dramatic gesture Cyrus found his voice and spoke. The action he had taken, he said, was forced upon him. No other course was possible in the interests of the people and their children. The Arabs were irresistible; God wanted to bring the land of Egypt under their dominion. Either the Byzantines would come to terms with them or they must see the streets running with blood; and after the massacre the survivors would have to forfeit all their possessions. The capitulation secured life, property and respect for the Christian religion, Melkite and Coptic alike. All those who preferred to live under a Christian government were free to leave Alexandria. Cyrus was moved to tears as he beseeched the people to believe him that he had done his best and made the treaty for their deliverance.

The tearful appeal of the aged patriarch stopped the rioters in their tracks. He looked old and pathetic, like an obsolete fortress with weapons all out of date, and there was not much due to him but pity. Some in the crowd even felt ashamed. Popular opinion swung around and the mob dispersed. The citizens not only furnished the instalment of tribute, but added to it a large sum of gold. The money was placed on board a vessel, which left the city by the southern gate and was delivered by Cyrus himself to the cavalry commander. This sealed the surrender of Alexandria. The first payment of tribute took place on 10 December 641.[9]

The ratification of the treaty with the Arabs was possibly the last act of emperor Heraclonas, whose reign ended that November. With Alexandria in captivity the cause of the empire was now quite hopeless. Only a few towns north of the Delta stood loyal to their colours; 'Amr was free to move against them at a time of his own choosing. He had resolved to build a new Muslim city in the plain, which stretched from the Roman fortress to the Mukattam Hills at the place of his encampment. According to Baladhuri, Zubair was first to build himself a house, in which he kept the ladder he used in scaling Babylon (it eventually perished in a fire). The architects of the town were Copts as the Arabs did not yet have the knowledge and art of planning towns.

The name Fustat, by which the town became known, was a source of perplexity for the Arab historians who wrote the history of the conquest two centuries later. Tradition had it related to 'Amr's tent (*fustat* in Arabic) and the story of the dove. It is also possible that the name originated from the Roman *fossatum*, which meant 'camp', or 'place of encampment'. From the beginning, it was also called Misr, a name that denoted Egypt as a whole, or Fustat-Misr. Today Fustat is embedded within greater Cairo and simply called 'old Cairo'.

At first, Fustat was not laid out on a large scale or with any idea of making it the Muslim capital. The earliest inhabitants lived in temporary shelters and it was only after the fear of war was removed from this part of the country that the Arabs could begin to build in durable materials. A common place of worship was their first necessity. A little to the south of the ramparts of Babylon, the oldest mosque in Egypt was built, the mosque of 'Amr. Its first foundation took place during the same winter of 641-2; the spot chosen was the one on which 'Amr had set up his standard.

The original mosque was a very simple building made of unbaked brick and measuring 17 by 29 metres (18 by 31 yards). Its prayer hall used palm trunks in place of pillars and it had no courtyard, no minaret and no *mihrab*, or niche, indicating the direction of prayer. The *kibla* wall that faced Mecca was built by eight of the Prophet's companions, chief among them Zubair and Ubayda. When the building was finished a *minbar* or pulpit was placed in it, and from there 'Amr delivered sermons, until Omar rebuked him for exalting himself above his fellow believers and ordered its destruction. Eventually mats were added in front of the small building over the pebble pavement and a chant to prayer instituted instead of beating a wooden gong. 'Amr's mosque was first rebuilt in 698 by the prefect of Fustat Abd el Aziz ibn Marwan and has since undergone numerous enlargements and additions, the latest in the 1990s (figs 30, 31).

From Fustat 'Amr could organize his marches against the northern towns, which had disputed the terms of surrender, Ikhna, Baralus, Balhib, Khais and Tinnis. He took them with little resistance. The surrender of Upper Egypt was consolidated by a separate column led by Kharija.

Alexandria itself was crowded with refugees, who had taken shelter behind its walls. By the terms of the treaty Byzantine solders and settlers within the walls were free to leave by land or by sea. No provision had been made for the Egyptians; as they beheld the constant flow of vessels bound for Cyprus, Rhodes and Constantinople they became restless and asked Cyrus to intervene with 'Amr to allow them to return to their villages. Their leave was refused. As most of them came from the Delta there was danger of their carrying arms to some of the unconquered towns.

Cyrus himself was a broken man. All the news from Constantinople was against him. Martina and her sons had been put to death or put aside, and by the end of November Constans had been proclaimed sole emperor. The friendship of Cyrus with Martina was notorious, as was his guilt for the loss of Egypt. With all hopes of personal safety gone, Cyrus sank into a profound depression and became an easy victim to a bout of dysentery, which seized him on Palm Sunday. On the following Thursday, 21 March 642, he died. A successor in the Melkite patriarchate was duly appointed; the deacon Peter was clothed with the *pallium* and seated on the throne left vacant by Cyrus. But he had no jurisdiction beyond the city walls. All hope for aid from Byzantium had vanished.

The people of Alexandria were beginning to discover that their hopes for a settled government with fixed taxation were groundless. The interruption of the river and sea traffic as well as the departure of the wealthy nobles and merchants who had resolved to abandon their homes in Egypt made the new taxation bear heavily on those who remained. Depression and melancholy hung over the city during the last few weeks of the armistice. Many of the houses were left empty. The noise of departures from the quays diminished as vessel after vessel, laden with Byzantines and their goods, sailed north never to return. Many books from the Great Library and others in private collections were probably sent away at this time. The sea was open, the passage to Constantinople unhindered and the market price of the books considerable. People would have keenly appreciated their value and secured their removal while there was still time, rather than leaving them to the mercy of the desert warriors to whom the city was to be delivered. In the centuries to come books from Alexandria found their way to the imperial libraries of Byzantium, to the Greek monasteries and to the book markets of Constantinople and Smyrna.

At the beginning of September a great fleet was gathering in the Royal Harbour to remove the remaining legions of the imperial army. Theodore, who was appointed governor of Egypt after the death of Cyrus, personally

30. Mosque of 'Amr, exterior. Fustat (old Cairo).

31. Mosque of 'Amr, courtyard.

undertook the mission of arranging for the withdrawal of the Byzantine forces from the Delta. The Nile was now rising high and all the waterways were available for transport. It was the month agreed on for the evacuation and with its arrival the remnant of the Byzantine garrisons embarked on military vessels and did not look back. On 14 September, the anniversary of the service of the Exaltation of the Cross, as hymns were sung in the Caesareum, the last orders for embarkation were issued. Three days later, on 17 September, Theodore's fleet cast off its moorings and set sail for Cyprus.

On 29 September eleven months of the armistice expired. The great gates of Alexandria were flung open and 'Amr rode at the head of his desert warriors, past the gleaming colonnades and the stately palaces of the Canopic Way. 'I have taken a city,' he wrote to Omar, 'of which I can but say that it contains 4,000 palaces, 4,000 baths, 400 theatres, 12,000 greengrocers and 40,000 tributary Jews.' So ended the Byzantine Empire in Egypt.

Mirror of Pharos

Everything about Alexandria was new to the Arabs. The marble streets dazzled them with light, the temples and obelisks appeared to have been built by *jinn* (supernatural beings). Nor were they less amazed by the subterranean labyrinth of cisterns, many descending to a depth of five storeys. 'Alexandria is a city upon a city,' wrote Suyuti,[1] 'so full is it of columns loftier and larger that any to be seen elsewhere.' One warrior said: 'I have made the pilgrimage to Mecca sixty times, but if Allah had suffered me to stay a month in Alexandria and pray on its shores, that month would be dearer to me!' The Caesareum impressed them to such a degree that the word 'kaisariya' became the word for 'palace' in the Middle Ages; it is still used to describe the main street of Arab towns. The historian Masudi described the temple roof as 'a single block of marble hewn by a *jinn*' and offered the following explanation for this marvel: 'In the quarries it was easy to work before mid-day, for the marble was as soft as paste, but in the afternoon it became hard and intractable.'[2]

In front of the Caesareum stood two Egyptian obelisks,[3] the tallest pillars the Arabs had ever seen. Masudi claimed they rocked in the wind; Yakubi described them as 'standing on two brazen crabs with ancient inscriptions'; Ibn Rustah thought the figures represented 'scorpions, made of copper or brass'. The obelisks probably rested on platforms decorated with scarabs, the sacred beetles of ancient Egypt (fig. 47).[4]

With Ibn el Fakih began a strange confusion between the two obelisks and the great lighthouse of Pharos, which the Arabs called *el Manara* (it became the prototype for minarets, fig. 32).[5] He wrote: '*el Manara* of Alexandria stands on a crab of glass in the sea'; and again: 'it has two pillars standing on two images, one of brass and one of glass, the brazen image in the form of a scorpion and the glass image in the form of a crab'. By the time of Masudi the story had become a legend:

> The lighthouse was built on a foundation of glass in the form of a crab, on a tongue of land projecting into the sea. On top of the lighthouse were images of brass. One figure pointed its right hand to the sun, wherever it might be in the heavens, and lowered its hand as the sun sank; another pointed to the sea in the direction from which an enemy was approaching, and as the enemy drew near, it cried out in a terrible voice, which could be heard two or three miles away, and so alarmed the inhabitants.

32. Minaret of the mosque of Ibn Touloun, Cairo, ninth century. The design reproduces the three storeys of the Pharos Lighthouse.

The figure 'pointing to the sun' was probably a winged Hermes or Nike standing on top of the dome sheltering the lantern.

The Pharos, of course, was an entirely different monument. It was a solid structure towering into the air to a height of 300 feet and its vast foundations could have hardly rested on glass. The Arabs lavished great admiration on it. This is how Istakari described it: '*El Manarah*, founded on a rock in the sea, contains more than three hundred rooms, among which the visitor cannot find his way without a guide.' Ibn Hawkal added: 'It was built of hewn stones fitted together and fastened with lead: there is nothing like it on earth!' Makrizi wrote:

> It is said that whoever entered this lighthouse became distracted and lost his way, by reason of the number of chambers and storeys and corridors which it contained ... So it is reported that when the Moors arrived in Alexandria in the caliphate of al Muktadir with an army, a body of them entered the lighthouse on horseback and lost their way, till they came upon a crevice in the crab of glass upon which the structure was founded; and many of them fell through it and perished.[6]

Even more marvellous stories were told about the mirror, which many thought was the greatest wonder of all. It projected a beam 30 miles out to sea, designed to guide arriving ships to the two harbours of Alexandria. To the Arabs, who had no experience in seafaring, the mirror appeared as an object of obscure magical power. Masudi described it as 'large, of transparent stone, in which ships could be seen coming from el Roum at too great a distance for the naked eye to detect them'. Makrizi wrote that it was made of 'finely wrought glass',[7] whereas Suyuti described the material as 'polished steel or Chinese iron'. All three agreed that it showed vessels at sea far beyond the range of human vision. Makrizi described its size as measuring up to 'five spans in diameter' and wrote that it was used as a burning glass to destroy enemy ships. Suyuti claimed that it was 'seven cubits wide' and confirmed the opinion that it was used as a burning glass: 'They turned the mirror towards the westering sun and the rays being reflected burned up the enemy ships.' Abdallah, the son of 'Amr, said: 'One of the Wonders of the World is the mirror hanging in the *Manara* of Alexandria, which shows what is passing at Constantinople.'[8]

As for seafaring, this is how 'Amr described a ship in a letter to Omar:

> Verily I saw a huge construction, upon which diminutive creatures mounted. If the vessel lies still, it rends the heart; if it moves, it terrifies the imagination. Upon it a man's power ever diminishes and calamity increases. Those within a ship are like worms in a log. If it rolls over, they are drowned; if it escapes peril, they are confounded.[9]

His description was said to have discouraged caliph Omar from seafaring. 'Put no water between yourselves and me,' he told his lieutenants. 'When

I travel to you from Medina, my horse must take me directly to the place where I join you.'

The most splendid part of the city was the *Brucheion*, the Royal Quarter. Although Aurelian had set it on fire in 273,[10] the ruins had been repaired during the three subsequent centuries, and John of Nikiu has described the magnificent eastern wall that was still standing at the time of the Arab conquest. Adjacent to the wall was the temple known as the Tetrapylus, an open pavilion with four rows of columns where Bishop Alexander had laid to rest the bones of the Prophet Jeremiah. This place was held in great veneration by John Moschus who described it in his work *Pratum Spirituale* (cap. 77). Close by stood the Church of St Mary Dorothea and further east, near the walls and the shore, that of St Mark with the marble shrine containing the bones of the apostle himself.[11] In the same part of town were the churches of St Theodore and St Athanasius.[12]

Serapeum Hill presented another wonder. Masudi described it as 'a great palace without equal on earth, standing on a large mound opposite the gate of the city. In the palace were 100 pillars made of different marble, polished like mirrors, so that a man could see in them who was walking behind him. In the midst of the hall was a pillar 111 cubits high.' By the time of the Arab conquest the temple of Serapis had been destroyed and only the small Church of St John the Baptist marked the spot. But the porticoes and outer colonnades of the temple were still visible as well as a beautiful marble fountain. Two more churches of Sts Cosmas and Damian and the *Angelion*[13] had been added in Christian times. Above the fortress towered the red granite column of Diocletian.

The Arabs called Diocletian's column 'Amud el Sawari and believed it to be part of a temple built by Solomon. Ibn el Fakih wrote that if a man threw some pottery or glass against it with the words: 'By Solomon, son of David, break in pieces,' then it broke, but without the talisman it did not. Suyuti claimed that if people closed their eyes and walked towards the pillar, they would always fail to reach it; he had tried it himself on three occasions and found it to be true. He also thought that on top of Diocletian's column stood a dome under which Aristotle used to study astronomy.

To the west of the fortress stood the amphitheatre, which Makrizi claimed 'held a million spectators, so arranged that one and all, from the highest tier of the seats to the lowest, could see all that went on and hear every word uttered without any crushing or inconvenience.' He also mentioned a hippodrome outside the eastern gate and a smaller theatre in the *Brucheion* (fig. 33).

The Arabs were most impressed by the defensive walls that followed the curving seashore on the north and rested on a canal in the east. The canal flowed into the city (it was here that the Persians had made their entry). All around, on every side, towers and bastions backed up the construction. The walls appeared to be impregnable, something that would come to haunt 'Amr and his warriors in the days to come.

33. Roman theatre on the hill of Kom el Dik opposite the railway station, Alexandria.

34. Roman and Arab city walls in Shallalat Gardens, Alexandria.

'Amr had every intention of making Alexandria his capital, but caliph Omar had heard enough about its wonders. His warriors were beginning to forget themselves and he had made up his mind that the new capital would be at Fustat. During the eleven months of armistice a settled government for the entire Nile valley had already been established; when 'Amr entered Alexandria he only had to provide for the administration of the city. Furthermore, Omar had poured a steady stream of reinforcements into Egypt swelling the strength of the Arab army. 'Amr now had at his disposal a large body of troops, apart from those required to garrison the main towns. Thus Omar sent explicit orders to 'Amr to leave Alexandria. 'Amr decided to undertake an expedition to Pentapolis in Cyrene, the next westward province of the Byzantine Empire.

In the seventh century stations were dotted along the whole route between Alexandria and Cyrene and much of the way lay through fertile country. The march was an easy one for the Arab horsemen and no opposition was encountered. Barca (Tolometa) capitulated under treaty at once, agreeing to pay 13,000 *denarii* as yearly tribute.[14] From Barca 'Amr continued to Tripolis, which was better fortified and had a larger Byzantine garrison. The city shut its gates and for some weeks withstood the Arab blockade.[15] Although the sea was open, no relief came from Byzantium and when the garrison was worn out by hunger, the Arabs entered the city through the unfortified harbour side of the wall. As the shouts of 'Allahu Akbar' rang through the streets, panic seized the people, who took what goods they could carry, ran to the ships and hoisted sail. The gates were abandoned and 'Amr entered unhindered with the bulk of the army.

Moving with characteristic swiftness 'Amr next surprised the city of Sabra (Roman Sabrata, modern Zurara) dashing upon it early in the morning. The people expected the Arabs to be at Tripoli and were completely unprepared; the city fell at the first onset. It was taken by force of arms and plundered. This marked the end of the rapid campaign.

Alexandria Lost

In the summer of 643 'Amr returned to Babylon and began building a fortress at Giza. The work was finished by November of that year. The country was settling down to a peaceful government and 'Amr was able to stay in Fustat. He sent a description of Egypt to caliph Omar, written in rhymed prose:

> Know, O commander of the faithful, that Egypt is a dusty city and a green tree. Its length is a month and its breadth ten days. It is enclosed by a barren mountain range and yellow sands. The Nile traces a line through its midst: blessed are the early morning voyages and its travels at eventide! It has its season for rising and for falling, according to the course of the sun and the moon. It causes milk to flow, and brings cattle in abundance. When the springs and fountains of the land are loosened, it rolls its swelling and sounding waters till the fields are flooded on both sides. Then there is no escaping from village to village save in little boats, and frail skiffs, and rafts as light as fancy or the evening mist. After the river has risen to its full measure, it sinks again to its former level. Moreover, the people, who are devout in worship, have learned to plough the earth well and truly and to hasten the seed time, trusting that the Most High will give them increase and will grant the fruit of their labour, though the labour is slight. So the crop is grown and streams of water bring on the harvest as moisture from beneath gives nourishment. At one time, Egypt is a white pearl; then golden amber; then a green emerald; then an embroidery of many colours.[1]

'Amr had fallen under Egypt's spell.

Having promised to honour the Christians, he called on the exiled Coptic patriarch Benjamin to take up his post. The Muslims had no interest in the truth or falsity of Chalcedon; when the monks of Wadi el Natrun declared their allegiance to 'Amr, he sent a bill of immunity to Benjamin. The message was delivered to Benjamin by word of mouth from Wadi el Natrun all the way to Upper Egypt.

Benjamin had spent thirteen years in hiding. To evade those in power and defy the odds for the sake of faith had become a way of life. The monks had wholeheartedly reassured him of 'Amr's good intentions and pointed out the advantages of being on his good side, but Benjamin made his way gingerly amid the familiar but altered landmarks of his youth. It was a time of uncertainty; everything depended on the good will of the Muslims.

Once again in this extraordinary story we are reminded of the power that individuals can exert on history. Benjamin and 'Amr liked each other as soon as they met. Benjamin felt that 'Amr's simple and direct manner inspired trust. After years of oppression and betrayal by his fellow Christians, this Muslim, a follower of another Prophet, treated him as an equal and a brother in arms. For his part, 'Amr said about Benjamin: 'In all the countries I have conquered up to this day, I have never seen a man of God like this.' They struck up a personal friendship that had profound consequences for the future of the Coptic Church.

'Amr asked Benjamin's advice on what was the best way of keeping the country in order and of raising revenue. Benjamin laid down five conditions: (1) that taxes should be collected at the right time, at the end of the agricultural season; (2) that no taxes should be demanded after the vintage had been collected; (3) that the canals should be dug out every year; (4) that the dykes and sluice gates should be kept in repair; and (5) that no unjust or tyrannical officials should be appointed. 'Amr was so impressed with Benjamin's intelligence and honesty that he offered his own guards to deliver him to Alexandria in safety.

After thirteen years of exile Benjamin returned to Alexandria in triumph. His restitution saved the Coptic Church from crisis if not destruction. Though there was little prospect of bringing back to the fold all those who had converted to Islam, many who had been driven by force to the Melkite Church could return.

Nevertheless, conversion to Islam had been considerable. It would not be fair to attribute this defection only to motives of material advantage. The offer of brotherhood with the conquerors and of freedom from tribute was powerful enough to sweep along a tide of converts. Many may have been sick of a Christianity out of which all love and hope had vanished in the sectarian wars – a Christianity that had betrayed its founder – and sought refuge in the calm and simplicity of Islam.

After the persecution the Copts had suffered at the hands of Cyrus, it would not have been surprising if they had wanted to retaliate. But 'Amr discouraged any such ideas; his government was impartial between the two forms of religion. All Christians enjoyed equal protection from the conquerors. The status of a protected people was created by the Treaty of Peace, by which the Christians obliged themselves to pay tribute in return for security and protection against foreign enemies. The binding conditions were these: (1) the Quran was not to be reviled nor copies of it burned; (2) the Prophet was not be called a liar nor spoken of contemptuously; (3) the religion of Islam was not to be condemned nor any attempt made to refute it; (4) no Christian was allowed to marry a Muslim woman; (5) no attempt was to be made to persuade Muslims against their religion, to injure them physically or materially; (6) the enemies of Islam were not be assisted, nor the rich among them entertained.

There were six more contingent conditions: (1) Jewish and Christian subjects had to wear distinctive garments with a girdle fastened around the waist; (2) their houses were not allowed to be built higher than those of the Muslims; (3) the sound of their bells[2] was not be forced on the ears of the Muslims, nor their reading or chanting, nor their opinions and their peculiar tenets, whether Jewish or Christian; (4) crosses were not to be displayed nor wine drunk in public, nor were pigs to be seen; (5) the dead were to be mourned in private and buried in private; (6) subjects had to ride only common horses and mules, not thoroughbreds.[3]

The tribute, which the Arabs called *jizrah*, was fixed at two *denarii* a head and was not levied on old people, women, children, slaves, madmen or beggars. It also seems that the population was divided into three classes and that each was assigned a different proportion of tribute, according to land and property owned.[4] The revenue raised by 'Amr after the settlement was 12,000,000 *denarii*.

There is some obscurity concerning the status of Alexandria. We know from historical accounts that the Alexandrians complained bitterly under the new system. This may be due to the loss of the privileged immunity from poll-tax, which they had previously enjoyed, and to the fact that the city suffered greatly by the loss of the sea trade and the departure of the wealthy merchants. Nevertheless, the early government of 'Amr was animated by a spirit of justice, even sympathy for the Egyptians. 'Amr maintained the civil administration of Egypt unaltered; he simply took over and directed the machinery, which he found in working order. Many Byzantine officials kept their posts after converting to Islam; the vacancies created by the departure of those who had chosen to leave were filled with Coptic Christians.

It is curious to see with what vitality Roman titles persisted under Arab rule. At the end of the seventh century a registrar was called a *chartularius*, his superior an *eparchos* or *archon*, the governor's residence was a *praetorium*, and the governor of Alexandria an *augustal*.[5] The term *dux* was used in several eighth-century legal documents[6] and by the tenth-century writer Severus.[7]

In spite of his enlightened rule 'Amr received little encouragement from caliph Omar in Medina. The relations between the two of them had become tense, as indicated by some of their correspondence.[8] Omar wrote:

I have been thinking about you and your condition. You find yourself in a great and splendid country, whose inhabitants God has blessed in number and power by land and by water. It is a land, which even the pharaohs, in spite of their unbelief, brought by useful works to a state of prosperity. I am therefore greatly astonished that it does not bring in half of its former revenue, although this falling cannot be excused by reason of famine or failure of the crops. Moreover, you have written of many taxes, which you have laid upon the country. I hoped now that they would come to me, instead of which you bring excuses, which have no meaning. I shall surely take no less than was formerly paid[9] ... Now I see that it is your bad administration, which hinders you. But, by the help of God, I have means to compel you to render me what I demand!

'Amr answered by admitting that under the pharaohs, who gave great attention to agriculture, Egypt was more productive than now, under the rule of the Muslims, but he protested about the unkind words:

> I have served the Apostle of God and his successor Abu Bakr; I have answered to the trust reposed in me, and I have rendered towards my caliph the duty which God laid upon me ... Now take back the governorship which you have given me, for God has kept me free from the avarice and meanness with which you have charged me in your letters ... You could have not said worse of a Jew of Khaibar. God forgive you and me.

Omar replied: 'I did not send you to Egypt in order to sate your lusts and those of your people, but because I hoped you would by good administration increase our revenue. Therefore upon receipt of this letter send me the taxes: for I have people here in great need.' 'Amr begged for respite until the harvest. He explained that he could not raise a large revenue without injustice to the people and that it was better to be merciful to them than to oppress them.[10] But Omar had heard enough: he replaced 'Amr as governor of Egypt by Abdallah ibn Sa'ad, who had served in Upper Egypt and the Fayoum. Abdallah contrived to wring another 2,000,000 *denarii* from the Egyptians, raising the sum to 14,000,000. 'The milk-camel gives more milk than in your time,' wrote the caliph. 'Yes,' 'Amr replied, 'and the reason is that you are starving her young.'

Muslims were at first forbidden to acquire land in Egypt – the land grants were very few.[11] They were meant to remain as soldiers, not landed settlers. But as the permanence of the occupation became clear to everyone this restriction was withdrawn and they became landowners. The land they acquired remained subject to land-tax that was no different from the one imposed on Copts. Poll-tax, however, was a different matter; it was a sign of subjection and unbelief. The adoption of Islam cancelled the poll-tax, and thus there was a direct premium placed on the change of religion; it had become a way of bribing the Christians to convert. As soon as Christians converted, they were exempt from poll-tax; this system had the obvious effect of crippling the state revenues. As the public exchequer became impoverished, new methods of taxation had to be devised.

In order to obtain more revenue Abdallah had increased the proportion of taxes to be paid by the Alexandrians. The burden of new taxation became impossible for them to meet and people despaired. The large underclass of sailors, harbour attendants, porters and servants had been left without work. There were no new sources of income. In distress, some of the leading men wrote letters to emperor Constans in Byzantium, asking him to intervene and deliver them from the Muslims. They pointed out that Alexandria was held by a very weak garrison, incapable of resisting the Byzantine army.

Constans had never forgotten the wound to the pride of the empire caused by the loss of Egypt. He promptly ordered general Manuel to command a contingent of the army and take Alexandria from the sea. Towards the end of 645[12] a great fleet of 300 ships sailed into the Royal Harbour. Only 1,000 Arabs had been left to defend the city; they were quickly overpowered and slain. Manuel's army not only took Alexandria unchallenged, but marched into the Delta, taking cities and levying the supplies of corn and money. Entire villages had sided with the Byzantines.

The Copts panicked; their sympathies were with the Arabs. The return of the Byzantines did not work in their favour: the question of their allegiance to Chalcedon was sure to come up again and reprisals against them follow for helping the Arabs. Once more Benjamin had to flee Alexandria and go into hiding. Furthermore, 'Amr had been recalled to Mecca and could not be called on to help.[13]

But as soon as news of the revolt in Alexandria reached Arabia 'Amr received immediate orders to resume the command of Egypt. He marched north and organized his men. For the last time the Byzantines encountered 'Amr and his army of 15,000 strong near Nikiu. A desperate battle took place under the walls of the fortress and on the canal of the river, which ran into town.

Both sides fought with signal valour. 'Amr was in the thick of combat and having had his horse wounded by an arrow was obliged to dismount and fight on foot. In one part of the field the Arabs were put to flight. At this point, a mounted Byzantine officer, who stood out by virtue of the magnificence of his armour inlaid with gold, shouted a challenge to the Arabs for single combat. One Humil, a humble-looking man of the tribe of Zubaid, took up the challenge; a long duel followed, sword against scimitar. The two armies paused to watch the encounter, shouting encouragement to the combatants. At last a fierce lunge made by the Byzantine was parried and returned with a blow from Humil's scimitar, which struck deep into the collar-bone of his adversary and killed him. Humil was himself covered with wounds and died almost immediately.[14] The battle was renewed with fresh fury, but it ended in the defeat of Manuel's forces, driven to retreat towards Alexandria. The broken army reached the capital in great disorder, hotly pursued by the Arabs, but they reached the walls in time to close the gates.

When 'Amr looked up at the impregnable walls of Alexandria, he said he had been foolish to leave them standing. And he swore that if he captured the city a second time he would level its walls to the ground.

The Arab camp was pitched on the eastern side of the walls; the engines of war, captured at Babylon, were mounted, Copts having volunteered to help operate them. 'Amr's army battered the walls until they effected a breach that was low and wide enough to permit entry. A popular medieval story claimed that an Alexandrian of Arab descent called Ibn Bisama opened the Gate of the Sun to the Arab army in return for his safety. This apocryphal tale may simply reiterate the Persian entry into Alexandria a century before; it is not confirmed by any of the historians.

Although it is not entirely clear where the entrance was made, it is certain that the city was taken by storm in the act of resistance and this time the Arabs rushed in, plundering, burning and slaying all before them. Nearly all that remained in the eastern quarter by the Gate of the Sun perished in the fire, including the Cathedral of St Mark.[15] The fighting went on until 'Amr put an end to it in the middle of the city; the place where he sheathed his sword was later marked by the Mosque of Mercy. This building no longer exists; it probably stood where Turkish Town turns towards Rhakotis in Sharia el Darda'a (fig. 35).[16]

Some of the Byzantine soldiers managed to reach the ships and put out to sea, but a great number perished in the city and Manuel himself was among the fallen. Women and children were taken as prizes of war. The second capture of Alexandria took place in the summer of 646.[17]

This time 'Amr gave the order to raze the walls of Alexandria to the ground. What remained was left in ruins and much of it was set on fire. The churches that still remained were converted to mosques. St Theonas became Djama' el Gharbi; St Athanasius became the Attarine Mosque (figs 36, 37). The latter was rebuilt by Sultan Hakim in 1004, with the Church of St Athanasius standing in the courtyard. During the nineteenth century it was mistakenly known to European travellers as the tomb of Alexander the Great because of a magnificent sarcophagus that stood in the garden; in 1801 the sarcophagus was taken by the English to the British Museum and identified as that of Nectanebo II (360-343 BC), the last native Egyptian pharaoh.

The city suffered the fate of a defeated enemy destined to be subordinate to the new capital, Fustat. In 811 the Arabs built new walls, but they enclosed only a fragment of the ancient city, vividly illustrating the decline of the population (fig. 34).

Next 'Amr turned his army against those towns in the Delta that had aided the rebellion. When they were taken, captives were sent to Medina. 'Amr was allowed to stay only one month in Alexandria after which he was to hand the city over to Abdallah.

In the interim 'Amr made another treaty with Benjamin. The Coptic patriarch had written to him, asking him not to vent his anger on the Copts, because it was not they who had broken the first treaty. He also asked to be buried in the Church of St John in Alexandria.[18] 'Amr reminded him of their friendship and graciously agreed to his terms.

The caliph was not blind to the great military talent of 'Amr and rewarded him by giving him the post of commander-in-chief of the army. Abdallah was to remain as governor. 'Amr refused with a caustic remark: 'I should be like a man holding a cow by the horns while another milked her.' For the second time he left Egypt.

Nine years later emperor Constans fitted out a second armada and sent it to reconquer Egypt. But by this time the Arabs had learned something of seamanship and their fleet intercepted the Byzantines. Though inferior in numbers and fighting capacity they baffled the Byzantine force which

35. A complex of restored mosques standing near 'Amr's original Mosque of Mercy, Alexandria.

was slow to react. Failure in battle was turned to disaster by a storm; the broken remnant of the great fleet was scattered and driven out to sea. From that moment on Muslim power in Egypt was not seriously menaced. Only the coast towns remained subject to isolated raids by Byzantine pirates.

As for 'Amr's own fortunes, he was made governor of Egypt once more in September 658 during the reign of caliph Mu'awiya. In January 662 Patriarch Benjamin passed away after a long illness. 'Amr said that he would soon follow; he survived Benjamin by exactly two years, during which he was kept busy organizing expeditions against the rebellious Berbers of Pentapolis.

We have an account of 'Amr's death from one of the army commanders in Pentapolis by the name of Ibn Abbas. When Abbas returned to Fustat in triumph from an expedition, he walked into 'Amr's house and found him ill in bed. He asked 'Amr how he felt and 'Amr told him he was dying. Ibn Abbas persisted: 'You have often remarked that you would like to find an intelligent man at the point of death, and to ask him what his feelings were. Now I ask *you* that question.' 'Amr replied: 'I feel as if heaven lay close upon the earth, and I between the two, breathing as through the eye of a needle.'[19] 'Amr died on Yum el Fitr AH 43, or 6 January 664, at the age of about 70. His body was carried in procession by his son Abdallah to the Mukkatam hills and we are told that he was buried at their foot, 'near the entrance to the ravine'. But the place of his grave has been forgotten; no mark or memorial survives.

36. The Attarine Mosque, eleventh century, Alexandria.

37. The Attarine Mosque, minaret.

The final legend associated with the Great Library of Alexandria was set during 'Amr's second capture of the city. The story as given by Barhebreus was well known in the Middle Ages and ran as follows. A certain John the Grammarian, a Christian priest who was on good terms with 'Amr due to his great learning, was said to have plucked up the courage to ask 'Amr about the fate of the library: 'You have examined the whole city and set your seal on every kind of valuable. I make no claim for anything that might be useful to you, but things useless to you may be of service to us.' 'What are you thinking of?' asked 'Amr. 'The books of wisdom,' said John, 'which are in the imperial treasuries.' 'That,' replied 'Amr, 'is a matter on which I can give no order without the authority of the caliph.' He wrote a letter to Omar, who answered thus: 'Regarding the books you mention: if what is written in them agrees with the Book of God, they are not required; if it disagrees, they are not desired. Destroy them therefore!' So 'Amr ordered the books distributed among the bathhouses of the city, where they provided fuel for the boilers for six months.

The story was recorded in the thirteenth century and is almost certainly a fabrication. The name of John the Grammarian is probably a reference to John Philoponus, the last philosopher of any renown in the city. At the time of 'Amr's second capture of Alexandria he would have been 120 years old. Many of the books in the Great Library were written on parchment and vellum and neither of these materials burns as fuel. Last but not least, the Christians destroyed the majority of the books 200 years before the Arabs arrived. What matters here is the moral of the story: the power of ignorance driven by faith ushered in 1,000 years of silence.

At the same time, there can be no doubt that some books from the Great Library became available to the Arabs. During the eighth and ninth century the Arabs made remarkable advances in medicine, physics, astronomy and biology. Arab scholars were familiar with the writings of Hippocrates, Galen, Euclid, Ptolemy and Archimedes as well as those of Plato and Aristotle. Alchemy of the Alexandrian variety, based on the so-called 'books of Hermes Trismegistus' that harked back to the ancient Egyptian religion, became all the rage among those interested in spiritual and esoteric pursuits. Arab writings of this period reveal thorough knowledge of these Hermetic texts, even some that have been lost since. In the eleventh century, the Persian traveller Nasir Khusraw described how at the Fatimid court in Cairo scholars studied the writings of the Neoplatonic philosophers of Alexandria.

What is less clear is how these books survived and how they came into Arab possession. Were books hidden? Were copies sold on the markets of Alexandria and Cairo in the centuries that followed the Arab conquest? The historical records on this subject are obscure; there were no Arab historians of Egypt in the seventh and eighth centuries and later writers were eager to suppress the story of the burning of the library. Nevertheless, the evidence suggests that some private and monastic libraries continued to exist.

We should bear in mind that the widespread use of codexes in Alexandria had encouraged the systematic production of numerous copies of famous works. A codex was composed of pages made of either papyrus or parchment and bound in a volume. Much more text could be included in a codex than on a roll and as a result several book-rolls were typically copied into a single codex, which often contained works by more than one author.[20] The custom of recopying books for personal use was introduced in Alexandria during the first century; by the third century the codex had entirely replaced the book-roll. The free circulation of codexes over the centuries would have increased the chance of survival of famous works; indeed some may have remained in Egypt after the Byzantines evacuated the country with all their possessions. The very fact that Alexandrian learning was not entirely extinguished implies the use of books. By the eleventh century the Arabs had produced their own polymaths such as al Kindi, al Farabi and Ibn Sina, later known in the west as Avicenna. When Latin translations of these texts emerged in southern Spain in the twelfth century they were eagerly studied at the first medieval universities in the west.

Books from Alexandria reached Europe from the Byzantine east as well. Numerous codexes were acquired for the Apostolic Library in the Vatican on the markets of Constantinople and Smyrna, and more were added to the collection when the Byzantines began streaming into Italy under pressure from the Turks. Among them, manuscripts preserving the works of the Alexandrian poets Callimachus and Theocritus, several books and epitomes of Polybius, works on mathematics and science by Euclid and Archimedes as well as the *Septuagint* edition of the Old Testament. Some manuscripts were only recently discovered in the Vatican Library: works by Menander (more popular than any other writer in Alexandria) that still await publication and a palimpsest – an erased and re-used manuscript – by Archimedes.[21] When the first printed editions of books appeared in Florence and Venice in the late fourteenth and early fifteenth centuries, they were styled on Byzantine copies of Alexandrian codexes.

Books survived randomly and in unusual ways. The Greek monk Maximus Planudes described finding an Arabic copy of Claudius Ptolemy's *Geographia* in the market of Constantinople in 1295. The book had come to the attention of the emperor Andronicus II Paleologus, who commissioned a Greek copy for himself. Eventually the Florentine patron Palla Strozzi persuaded a Byzantine scholar to translate Planudes' Greek into Latin. The book was then acquired for the Vatican Library and a copy of it commissioned by the court of Spain. The latter was said to have inspired Christopher Columbus to venture on his historic voyage. But sadly, it was not until the European Renaissance that interest in the exploration of the world was awakened once more.

Notwithstanding these fortuitous finds, we should not underestimate the seriousness of the destruction of the classical heritage. Nor should we assume that it was the best material that survived. Nearly all Hellenistic

38. A sphinx and 'Pompey's Pillar', Serapeum, Alexandria.

39. 'Pompey's Pillar', Serapeum, Alexandria.

40. Panorama of Turkish Town, built on top of the silted *Heptastadion* dyke, Alexandria.

41. Mosques in Turkish Town, Alexandria.

writings on science have perished. The Middle Ages favoured compilations, or at least books written in a language still understandable to a civilization that had returned to a pre-scientific stage. Thus we have Varro's work on agriculture and Vitruvius' on architecture, but not their Hellenistic sources. We have Lucretius' poem on nature, but not the works of Strato of Lampsacus, who according to the ancient authors had originated natural science in the true sense. Among the scientific works preserved by the Byzantines and the Arabs two criteria seem to have been at work: the first was to give preference to authors of the Roman Imperial Period whose writings were easier to use. The second was to select the more accessible works, and of these, only the initial portions. We have the Greek text of the first four, more elementary, books of Apollonius' *Conics*, but not the next four. Of these, three have survived in Arabic. We have Latin and Arabic translations of the work of Philo of Byzantium on experiments in pneumatics, but none of his works on theoretical principles.[22]

The same is true of history. There remains no sustained historical account of the period between 301 BC, when the *Biblioteca Historica* of Diodorus Siculus breaks off, and 221 BC, the beginning of Polybius' *Histories* that have also reached us incomplete. Not only do we have no historical works dating from the Hellenistic Period, but even the subsequent work of Livy is missing ten books, which described events that took place from 292 to 219 BC. Tradition had preserved the rise of Classical Greece and the rise of Rome, two periods that remained the cultural reference points for the early Middle Ages, whereas Hellenistic Alexandria was forgotten. In philosophy, a few papyrus fragments written by Chrysippus have been found in Herculaneum. That is all that remains of a hundred or so books of an author reputed to have been the greatest thinker of Hellenistic times.

The lighthouse of Pharos suffered serious injury within a century of the conquest. Ibn Touloun built a wooden dome on its summit in 875, an act which suggests that the building was no longer used as a lighthouse, but merely as a watchtower. When the dome was swept away by the winds, a small mosque was built in its place by Malik al Kamil. In the next century, on the tenth day of Ramadan, AH 344 (28 December 955) about 30 cubits of the top were thrown down by a severe earthquake, which was felt all over Egypt, Syria and North Africa.[23] In 1182 another mosque on the summit was described by Ibn Jubayr,[24] who gave the height of the tower as 'above 150 cubits', showing it had halved from its original height of 300 cubits. Yakut, who wrote some forty years after Ibn Jubayr, actually drew a diagram of the lighthouse, which showed a square building like a fort with a shortened second storey and a small dome above it. He added: 'all the stories about the great height of the Pharos are shameless lies ... I sought the place of the mirror and found no trace of it.' Another earthquake in 1375 demolished all but the lowest storey of the tower.

As for the disappearance of the mirror, the Arabs blamed the Byzantines for it. A popular story described how the Byzantines were alarmed at the advantage the Pharos had given the Arabs and resolved to destroy the mirror. One of the courtiers of the emperor went with rich presents to caliph el Walid and professed his desire to become a Muslim. He tempted the caliph's greed by telling him that there was a vast store of gold and jewels buried in the vaults and chambers of the Pharos. The caliph sent troops to conduct a search and his men pulled down half the lighthouse tower, removing the mirror. The mischief was done. The Arabs found nothing, tried rebuilding what they had destroyed brick by brick but couldn't raise the building to its former height. When they replaced the mirror, it was useless. Feeling angry and betrayed they cut it loose and it was smashed to pieces on the rocks beneath.

Alexandria, once home to the wonders of the world, continued to fall from grace as each new ruler built less memorable structures in layers over the ancient city. Much has been lost. The locations of the ancient Museion with its adjacent schools and the Great Library, of the original Church of St Mark and the Catechetical School, are not known; neither are those of the tomb of Alexander nor of any of the ancient streets described by so many visitors. Of the two gates of the Sun and the Moon there survives not even a description.

The marble columns on Serapeum Hill stood for several more centuries. A hundred years after the Arab conquest they were seen by Idrisi. In 1160 Benjamin of Tudela described how 'the school of Aristotle' stood on a hill in Alexandria, 'a large and beautiful building with columns of marble dividing the various halls'. In 1167, Alexandria's governor Kharaja, the vizier of Salah ed-Din (Saladin of the Crusades), had them broken down, taken to the shore and thrown into the sea to obstruct a crusader landing. From that day on Diocletian's column has risen in solitary grandeur as the only remnant of the remarkable group of buildings that stood on the acropolis of Alexandria (fig. 38). The crusaders called it 'Pompey's Pillar' and it is still mistakenly known by that name today (fig. 39). Pharos was turned into a fortress by Qaytbey, the fifteenth-century Mamluke Sultan of Cairo (fig. 46). It stands at one fifth of its original height. The heptastadion dyke has silted up; it is now a wide peninsula housing the Turkish Town (figs 40, 41).

Epilogue

The fortunes of the Copts rose and fell with the rulers of Egypt. At first, they received greater financial and religious freedoms under the Muslims than under the Byzantines, obtaining the status of *dhimmis*, protected non-Muslims. They also came to play an important role in government. At the same time, they became a subject people who were assessed an annual poll tax and suffered second-class citizenship, social restrictions and, eventually, persecution.

During the first century after the Arab conquest Copts continued to make up the vast majority of the population of Egypt; in the eighth and ninth centuries they began their decline to a minority people. Coptic revolts were crushed twice in the eighth century, a period that also saw a major migration of Arabs into Egypt. In the winter of 828/9 the Venetians stole the relics of St Mark and transferred them to Venice. According to a popular medieval legend, they concealed them from the Muslim officials by immersing them in a tub of pickled pork. In 831 the Bashmunite revolt was violently suppressed by the Arabs and a great wave of conversion of Copts to Islam took place.

By the end of the ninth century Copts were a large minority in Egypt and their percentage quickly decreased in the opening decades of the tenth century. Coptic remained the liturgical language of the Church, but as Arabic was now the language of government and business, more and more Copts became primarily Arabic speakers.

For the next century the Coptic patriarchate paid an annual tax of 1,000 *denarii*. As a result of this financial burden, simony, or the selling of ecclesiastical offices, was common until Pope Abraham (975-978) got the tax reduced. Under Salah ed-Din they were subject to severe social and ecclesiastical restrictions. In Alexandria, the Church of St John the Baptist on Serapeum Hill and the rebuilt Cathedral of St Mark were demolished to prevent Crusaders from launching attacks from them. Alexandria became a *taghr*, 'frontier-town', a fortress for the pursuit of Holy War against the Franks.

At the same time, its commerce, now turned towards the Arab world, came to life once again. Ibn Jubayr, an Arab traveller who visited Alexandria in the twelfth century, described it as the most beautiful and vibrant city he had ever seen:

> We saw no other city where the streets are so vast or the buildings so tall, or that is more beautiful or more full of life. Its markets are very busy. As for

the construction of the city, it is astonishing that the underground structures are as extensive as those on the surface and are as beautiful and solidly built. This is because the waters of the Nile flow underground beneath all the houses and streets. The wells thus adjoin one another and intercommunicate ...

Among the virtues and claims to fame of this city, credit for which is due to the Sultan, are the *madrasas* (schools) and monasteries reserved for students and the devout who flock here from distant lands. There everyone finds accommodation, a master to teach him the branch of knowledge he wants to study and a pension to provide for his needs. The Sultan cares so much for those special foreigners that he had baths installed which they use, and has founded a hospital where their sick are cared for.

It is curious that in this city the people have the same occupation night and day. This is also the city with most mosques to the point that any estimate is approximation only: some exaggerate their number, others underestimate them. They are indeed very numerous, four or five on the same spot and sometimes one comprises several.

Christian monasteries declined, but they continued to supply most of the Church's bishops and patriarchs. During the fourteenth century, when the Mamlukes came to rule Egypt, conversions to Islam increased and even regions in Upper Egypt that were staunchly Christian became mostly Muslim. Under the Ottomans (1517-1798) Copts continued to have difficulties. It has been estimated that at the end of the seventeenth century there were only about 150,000 Coptic Christians. The very existence of the monasteries came under serious threat: St Anthony dwindled from fifty monks to fifteen, St Macarius from twenty to four and St Bishoi from twenty-four to five.[1] With the Church in decline, the first modern reform came under Pope Cyril IV (1854-1861), who stressed education for the clergy and adherence to traditional liturgical practice.

In the twentieth century the Copts enjoyed a comeback, helped by the growth of the Coptic *diaspora*. Almost a million Copts live outside Egypt. They reside mainly in Britain, Canada, Australia and the United States. With financial help from the *diaspora* the Coptic Church has invested in developing social services for the people and ushered in the rebirth of monasteries and monasticism. From 1959 onwards the Coptic Church entered into ecumenical dialogues and took its place on boards and committees of the World Council of Churches. In 1968 Pope Cyril laid the foundation stone for the reconstruction of the shrine of St. Menas outside Alexandria and negotiated the translation of the relics of St Mark from Venice to Cairo. In Alexandria, the new Cathedral of St Mark was built off Sharia Horreya, opposite Sharia Nebi Daniel (fig. 42). An inscription inside the cathedral claims that the remains of all the patriarchs of the Coptic Church are buried there, but this is hardly likely considering how often the cathedral had changed its location. Today the Copts in Egypt number some 8 million people and constitute 10 per cent of Egypt's population. They maintain the status of a protected minority.

42. Contemporary mosaic of St Mark writing the Gospel with a lion at his feet, an angel guiding his hand and the Pharos Lighthouse in the background. The new Cathedral of St Mark, Alexandria.

125

43. The French army in battle with the Mamlukes, etching by Vivant Denon, 1802.

44. Sketches of Egyptian, Greek and Arab faces, etching by Vivant Denon, 1802

45. Equestrian statue of Mohammed 'Ali, Mansheya Square, Alexandria.

46. Fort Khayt Bey, built on top of the lower storey of the ancient Pharos Lighthouse, Alexandria.

47. One of the obelisks that stood in front of the Caesareum, photograph taken in the nineteenth century.

48. The bay of Alexandria.

With Napoleon's invasion of Egypt in 1798 Alexandria re-entered the sphere of European politics (figs 43, 44). During the rule of Mohammed 'Ali (1769-1849) the city's commerce rose with the cotton trade and a new cultural renaissance took place (fig. 45). Alexandria became a modern cosmopolitan hub, drawing people from all over the world. It was a second golden age: for more than a century the city went on to inspire artists, architects and writers of all nationalities who immortalized its nostalgic, evocative spirit. The revolution of 1956 ushered in a new phase. During Nasser's rule the foreign communities left once again and since then the city has seen a massive increase in population. Today it houses some five million people and it is still the largest city on the Mediterranean coast (fig. 48).

The ecclesiastical life of Alexandria is not as intense today as it was in the days of Athanasius and Cyril, but it is even more complicated. The city is home to four patriarchates: the Greek, the Armenian, the Coptic and the Latin. In addition, it houses the Syrian Greek, the Greek Catholic, the Maronite, the Armenian Catholic, the Chaldean Catholic, the United Presbyterian and the Church of England. The majority of the population is Muslim.

Appendix

Texts

Philo Judaeus, Embassy of the Jews of Alexandria to Caius Caligula in Rome, quoted in Josephus. Description of the Caesareum:

It is a temple incomparable above all to others. It stands by a most commodious harbour, wonderfully high and large in proportion, an eminent sea mark, full of choice paintings and statues with gifts in abundance; and then it is beautiful all over with gold and silver; the model curious and regular in the disposition of the parts, as galleries, libraries, porches, courts, halls, walks and consecrated groves, as glorious as expense and art could make them; and everything in its proper place; besides that, the hope and comfort of seafaring men, either coming in or going out.

The Nicene Creed

We believe in one God, the Father Almighty, maker of all things, visible and invisible. And in our Lord, Jesus Christ, the Son of God, begotten of the father, God of God and Light of Light, very God of very God, begotten, not made, being of one substance with the Father, by whom all things were made in Heaven and on Earth, who for us and for our salvation came down and was made flesh, made man, suffered and rose again on the third day, went up into the heavens and is to come again to judge the quick and the dead;

and in the Holy Ghost;

but the Holy Catholic and Apostolic Church anathematizes those who say that there was a time when the Son of God was not, and that he was not before he was begotten, and that he was made from that which did not exist; or who assert that he is of other substance or essence than the Father, or is susceptible of change.

Mohammed's letter to Heraclius

I begin with the name of Allah, the Compassionate, the most Merciful. From Mohammed ibn Abdullah, the Messenger of God, to Heraclius, the emperor of Rome. Peace be upon him who follows our guidance. I call you to Islam. Accept Islam and you will be safe. God will give you your reward double-fold. If you forsake the message of God, you will carry the sin of all your followers. Say: O, people of the book! Come to common terms between us and you: that we worship none but Allah, that we associate no partners

131

with Him; that we elect not from among ourselves lords and patrons other than Allah. If they turn their back say: Bear witness that we are Muslims (submitting to Allah's will).

Ancient and medieval writers (in chronological order)

Polybius (203-120 BC) was a Greek historian of the Hellenistic Period born in Arcadia in Greece. He wrote the *Histories*, which covered the period from 220 to 146 BC, and was well known for his views about political balance in government, some of which have been drafted into the US constitution.

Strabo (63/64 BC-AD 24) was a Greek historian, geographer and philosopher born in Amaseia in Pontum (modern Amasya in Turkey), which had fallen under Roman rule not long before his birth. Taking advantage of the *Pax Romana* of the Augustan age, Strabo travelled to Egypt as far south as Philae *c.* 25 BC. He completed his *Geography* in Rome during the final years of his life.

Josephus (AD 37-*c.* 100) was also known as Yusef Ben Matiyahu, and as Titus Flavius Josephus after he became a Roman citizen. His two most important works are *The Jewish War*, written *c.* 75, and *Antiquities of the Jews*, written *c.* 94. The latter recounts the history of the world from a Jewish perspective; both works provide valuable insight into the Judaic and Christian religions of that age.

Zacharias of Mitylene (dates not certain), also known as Zacharias Scholasticus and Zacharias Rhetor, was an ecclesiastical historian who wrote a history of the Church covering the years 450-91.

John Moschus (550-619) was a Syrian monk and a writer about Christian asceticism. He was born in Damascus and lived in the monastery of St Theodosius in Jerusalem, where he acquired the nickname 'The Abstemious'. He also spent time with hermits in the Jordan Valley and at St Sabas Monastery near Bethlehem. In 578 he went to Egypt and travelled in the Delta, as far west as the Great Oasis (Siwa). After 583 he spent almost ten years on Mount Sinai. In 614-15, he went to Cyprus and from there to Rome, where he died in 619. On his deathbed he asked to be buried on Mount Sinai or in the monastery of St Theodosius. At the time Egypt was under Arab rule, and he was buried in Jerusalem. His best-known work, *Pratum Spirituale*, or 'Spiritual Meadow', is an account of his travels and personal experiences. He also wrote a life of John the Almoner, together with Patriarch Sophronius of Jerusalem. A fragment of this has been preserved by Leontias of Neapolis under the name 'Simeon Metaphrastes'.

John, Bishop of Nikiu, served as bishop during the reigns of the Coptic Patriarchs John of Samanud, Isaac and Simeon (680-701). He is the author of the *Chronicle*, which begins with the creation of Adam and ends with the Arab conquest of Egypt. The *Chronicle* is especially noteworthy for its passages describing events in the seventh century that are not known from other sources. Although John was not an eyewitness, he was of the generation immediately following the conquest and he is the only near contemporary whose account has come down to us. His chronology is not always consistent, but his information and detail are vivid.

John was a Coptic Monophysite and his interpretation of the historical events is consistent with his persuasion: he describes the Islamic conquest of Egypt as a divine chastisement of the Byzantines for the Chalcedonian 'heresy'. The *Chronicle* was originally written in Greek, with some chapters in Coptic, judging by the forms of the names. The work survives only in an Ethiopian translation made in 1602 from an Arabic version of the original. A passage covering thirty years from 610 to 640 is missing and the text is corrupted by various other omissions.

Eutychius or Sa'id ibn Batriq (876-940) was born in Fustat. He became one of the first Arabic Christian writers, best known for his extensive *Annals*, a world chronicle. He did not speak Greek but was able to access the Greek texts in Syriac translation. In 932 he became the Melkite Patriarch of Alexandria at the age of 60, probably due to the influence of the Muslim rulers. His appointment met with considerable opposition, which lasted for the rest of his life.

El Tabari, Abu Jafar Muhammed ibn Jabir (838-923) was one of the earliest and most prominent Persian historians and exegetes of the Quran who wrote exclusively in Arabic. He was born in Amol, Tabaristan and travelled to Syria, Palestine and Egypt. He spent much of his life in Cairo, where he became part of the 'famous four' – Ibn Jarir, Ibn Khuzayma, Ibn Harun and Ibn Nasr – all well respected scholars of their day. He died in Baghdad.

El Masudi, Abu el Hassan 'Ali ibn el Hossein ibn 'Ali (896-956) was an Arab historian and geographer born in Baghdad. He was known as the 'Herodotus of the Arabs', having spent much of his life travelling in Armenia, Azerbaijan and the distant regions of the Caspian Sea, as well as in Syria, Arabia and Egypt. He also travelled to the Indus Valley, from where he sailed to East Africa. Although many of his writings have been lost, some 20 books attributed to him still remain. Masudi spent the last years of his life in Cairo.

Ibn Rusta (exact years not known) was a tenth-century Persian explorer and geographer, born in the Rusta district of Isfahan. He wrote a geographical compendium.

Barhebreus or Abu el Faraj ibn Harun el Malati (1226-1286) was a bishop of the Syriac Orthodox Church, noted for his works on philosophy, poetry, language, history and theology. He has been called 'one of the most learned and versatile men of his time'. Trained in medicine, he pursued many other branches of knowledge, which he did not abandon until the end of his life. He was respected by all the Christian factions and at his death mourned by Nestorians and Armenians alike. He was buried at the convent at Mar Matthew near Mosul.

Ibn Khaldoun, Abu Zaid 'Abdel Rahman bin Muhammed ibn Khaldoun el Hadrami (1332-1406) was born in North Africa, present day Tunisia. He was a polymath who excelled in many disciplines and is considered to be the forerunner of the social sciences and modern economics by anticipating many elements in these disciplines centuries before they were founded in the West. He is best known for his work *Muqqadima* or *Prolegomenon*, as it was called in the West, his first volume of a book on universal history. He spent the last years of his life in Cairo, acting as a teacher and judge.

El Makrizi or Taqi ed-Din Ahmad ibn 'Ali ibn 'Abd el Khadir ibn Muhammed el Makrizi (1364-1442) was an Egyptian historian of the Mamluke Period born in Cairo. He was trained in the Hanifite school of law and became a renowned scholar and lecturer, writing some 200 works. The most important of these is considered to be *el Khitat*, which was translated into French in 1854 as *Descriptions topographiques et historiques de l'Égypte*.

Ibn Hajar (1372-1448) was a scholar of the Mamluke Period born in Cairo. He wrote more than fifty historical works and achieved great fame during his lifetime. He rose to the position of Chief Judge (Qadi) of Egypt.

Abu el Mahasin (d. 1469) was a pupil of el Makrizi who continued his teacher's *History of Egypt* from its conclusion in 1441 until his own death in 1469.

El Suyuti, Imam Jalaluddin (1445-1505), also known as Ibn Khutab, 'the son of books', was born in Cairo. He was a writer, religious scholar, expert on law and teacher whose works addressed a variety of subjects. He was appointed as chair in the mosque of Sultan Baybars in Cairo.

Fayoum portraits

In the 1880s, a large collection of ancient portraits that was in the hands of an Austrian dealer reached the western art markets. They were an instant sensation. Many found their way into museum collections even though their exact provenance was uncertain. They were known to have come from Egypt because the British archaeologist Flinders Petrie had excavated a number of them in Hawara and Philadelphia in the Fayoum Oasis; hence their name. They constitute the most outstanding body of painting to have come down to us from the ancient world. They are painted in encaustic (heated beeswax mixed with pigments) in the Greek tradition, while being designated for Egyptian-style burials. The two-dimensional portrait of the deceased, called *eikon*, was a substitute for the traditional Egyptian mummy mask. Beeswax dries rapidly and the portrait was painted swiftly and impressionistically during the sitter's youth or prime of life. It was then inserted into the mummy shroud over the face before burial. The immediacy and naturalism of these portraits had prompted André Malraux to describe them as glowing with the flame of immortal life. The Fayoum portraits point to the existence of a great school of painting, the memory of which has been lost. It was probably based in Alexandria. The late classical style of the paintings with their enlarged eyes that look directly at the viewer provided a model for the first Christian icons.

Vivant Denon

Two illustrations in this book come from Vivant Denon's *Travels in Upper and Lower Egypt*, published in 1802. Dominique-Vivant Denon (1747-1825) was invited to accompany Napoleon Bonaparte during the French expedition to Egypt (1799-1801). He soon became known as 'Napoleon's eye' and the primary force behind revealing Egypt's civilization to an astonished Europe. He was the first to systematically record and describe the monuments of Egypt and to combine his scholarly record with informed observations about the people he encountered. With often a few minutes to record the scene before him, he would sketch rapidly. On one occasion he worked for sixteen hours while the windblown sand caused his eyelids to bleed. He published his notes and drawings as soon as he returned to France, describing a culture long shrouded in darkness and mystery. His book became an instant bestseller. Denon was rewarded for his services by being made a Baron and becoming the first director of the Louvre. Twenty years later he collaborated on the *Descriptions de l'Égypte*, a book that became one of the pillars of the nascent field of Egyptology. Denon was also an architect; he contributed to the creation of the *Arc de Triomphe* and the design and ornament of a number of squares in Paris.

Chronology

Siege of Alexandria	June	641
Return of Cyrus to Egypt	September	641
Surrender of Alexandria	November	641
Death of Cyrus	March	642
Evacuation of Alexandria by the Romans	September	642
'Amr's expedition to Pentapolis	winter	642-643
Restoration of Benjamin	autumn	644
Revolt in Alexandria under Manuel	late autumn	645
Second battle of Nikiu	late spring	646
Arab conquest of Alexandria	summer	646
Recall of 'Amr from Egypt	autumn	646
Reinstatement of 'Amr as governor of Egypt	August	658
Death of Benjamin	3 January	662
Death of 'Amr	6 January	664

Roman emperors

Aurelian	270-275
Probus	276-282
Diocletian	284-305
Maximian	286-305
Galerius	305-311
Constantius	293-306
Constantine I	306-337
Maxentius	306-312
Maximinus Daia	305 (or 307)-313
Licinius	308-324
Constantine II	337-340
Constans (co-ruler)	337-350
Constantius II (co-ruler)	337-361
Magnetius (co-ruler)	350-353
Julian the Apostate	361-363
Jovian	363-364
Valentinian I (west)	364-375
Valens (co-ruler, east)	364-378
Gratian (co-ruler, west)	375-383
Theodosius (co-ruler)	379-395
Valentinian II (co-ruler, west)	375-392
Eugenius (co-ruler)	392-394

Byzantine emperors

Arcadius	395-408
Theodosius II	408-450
Marcian	450-457
Leo I	457-474
Leo II	474
Zeno	474-491
Anastasius	491-518
Justin I	518-527
Justinian I	527-565
Justin II	565-578
Tiberius Constantine	578-582

Maurice	582-602
Phocas	602-610
Heraclius	610-641
Constantine III (co-ruler)	641
Heraclonas (co-ruler)	641

Melkite patriarchs

Theodore	609
John the Almoner	609-616 or 617
George	621-630 or 631
Cyrus	631-642
Peter	642-unknown

Coptic patriarchs

Anastasius	604-616
Andronicus	616-623
Benjamin	623-662
Agathon	662-680
John of Samanud	680-689
Isaac	690-693
Simeon	694-701

Notes

1. Alexander's City

1. Plutarch, *Greek Lives*, trans. R. Waterfield (Oxford, 1998), 306ff.
2. Quoted in A.J. Butler, *The Arab Conquest of Egypt – And the Last Thirty Years of the Roman Dominion* (Oxford, 1902), 369.
3. For a discussion of the parabolic mirror of Pharos see L. Russo, *The Forgotten Revolution* (Berlin and Heidelberg 2004), 117n.80.
4. G. Botti, *L'Acropole d'Alexandrie* (Alexandria, 1895), 7.
5. Polybius mentioned that the gates were added after the revolt of Cleomenes.
6. Suyuti wrote that a 'dome overlaid with brass, which shone like gold' still stood in the open shrine after the Arab conquest. Makrizi also wrote about a 'dome formed of one block of marble of the finest workmanship' in a circular temple on Serapeum Hill, as quoted in Butler, *op. cit.*, 385-7.They were probably describing the same building.
7. The Academy and the Lyceum in Athens had many features in common with it, but they were private institutions.
8. J.Y. Empereur, *Alexandria: Past, Present and Future* (London 2002), 35.

2. Christianity in Egypt

1. Possibly to the east of Silsileh.
2. It stood on the site of the present Franciscan church by the docks.
3. Bearing in mind how far Dendera is from the Nile Delta, the number may be somewhat exaggerated. Jerome is well known for his hyperbole.
4. See E. Pagels, *The Gnostic Gospels* (London 1980).
5. It was reopened in a different location in 1893.
6. See J. Kamil, *Coptic Egypt: History and Guide* (Cairo and New York 1993), 38.

3. The Arian Dispute

1. Quoted in H.A. Drake, *Constantine and the Bishops: The Politics of Intolerance* (Baltimore and London 2000) p. 240.
2. Constantine's motives for adopting the Christian faith and his practical, level-headed religious policies are discussed by C. Freeman, *The Closing of the Western Mind: The Rise of Faith and the Fall of Reason* (New York 2005), 154-78.
3. Later tradition asserted that there were 318 bishops present. The actual number was probably smaller; 318 was the number of the army which Abraham had gathered to rescue Lot in Genesis 14:14. It was an analogy used by later commentators to illustrate the point that orthodoxy was being rescued from the clutches of heresy.
4. C. Freeman, *op. cit.*, 167.
5. J. Pelikan, *The Christian Tradition* (Chicago and London 1971), vol. 1, 203.
6. The debate centered on the use of the word *homoousios*, 'of the same

141

substance (as God the Father)' introduced at Nicaea, and proposed to substitute it with a less offensive one: *homoios*, 'like (the Father)'. As Gibbon remarked, it was 'a furious contest over a single diphthong'.

7. N. McLynn, *Ambrose of Milan: Church and Court in a Christian Capital* (Berkeley, 1994), 106.

8. Those who had accepted the use of the word *homoios* of the Dated Creed as opposed to *homoousios*, introduced at Nicaea.

9. Quoted in J. McManners (ed.), *The Oxford Illustrated History of Christianity* (Oxford 1990), 137.

4. Hypatia and St Catherine

1. Some question whether the entire contents of the Daughter Library were destroyed on this occasion. However, Rufinus described the utter destruction of the whole building and the library was part and parcel of it.

2. *Chronicle* of John of Nikiu, cap. 84.87-103 (see Appendix).

3. *Chronicle* of John of Nikiu, though written in the late seventh century, was founded on earlier works that have perished.

4. John Moschus, *Pratum Spirituale* (Michigan 2006), cap. 172 (see Appendix).

5. Zachariah of Mitylene, *Chronicle* (London, 1889), 209 (see Appendix).

6. Zachariah of Mitylene, *Chronicle*, 101 (see Appendix).

7. They perished some time later; see E. Matter, *Ecole d'Alexandrie* (Paris 1840), vol. II, 381.

8. Barhebreus (Abu el Faraj), *Chronicon Ecclesiasticum* (Louvain 1872), 424 (see Appendix).

9. For a description of the Caesareum see Appendix.

5. The Persian Conquest

1. The Persian siege of Alexandria was described in the so-called *Syrian Chronicle*; see W. Wright, *Chronicle of Joshua the Stylite composed in Syriac AD 507* (Cambridge 1882).

2. At the beginning of his *Life of Benjamin* the historian Severus noted the preservation of Deir el Kibrius from the Persians. We know that Ennaton and its library escaped destruction because in 694 the Coptic patriarch Simon completed his theological studies there.

3. It was situated to the north of the modern Mahmoudiya canal.

4. The Alexandrian prisoners were later released after the victory of Heraclius at Dastagerd.

5. Trans. M. Amélineau, *Étude sur le Christianisme en Égypte au septième siècle* (Paris 1887), 30.

6. The conquest of Egypt seems to have taken at least three years; this fact complicates calculating the precise chronology of the Persian occupation.

7. Zachariah of Mitylene, *Chronicle*, 266.

8. According to Barhebreus, *Chronicon*, two more were later added by Sergius; it is not known whether this was the same Sergius who practised medicine in Rhesaina.

9. The canons of the Church did not allow the consecration of a patriarch under the age of 35.

6. Heraclius' Crusade

1. The quote was given by Theophanes. According to Butler, *op. cit.,* it was confirmed by Persian writers, see 119n.1.

2. Cedrenus places the peace arrangement to the eleventh year of Heraclius, i.e. 621 or 622.

3. Butler points out the fact that the cardinal blunder of the Persians was their lack of interest in learning how to fight on the sea (*op. cit.,* 121-2). For ten years they had sat in idle occupation of Chalcedon, Antioch and Alexandria. Sebeos (see R. Bedrosian, *Sebeos, Bishop of the Bagratid Princedom* (New York 1985) gives us the information that after sending his insolent letter, Chosroes equipped a large squadron and sent it out to sea to pursue the Byzantines, but the Byzantine galleys defeated the Persians so thoroughly that the Persians never again ventured to sea.

4. *Pace* Butler who places this incident before the capture of Dastagerd, some time during the year of 627. The letter is now kept in the Hashemiya palace near Amman, Jordan.

5. Muslim tradition holds it that Heraclius wanted to convert but was dissuaded by his advisors.

6. According to Sebeos the Jews had initially surrendered Jerusalem to the Persians; after a few months the Christians had rebelled and slain the Persian garrison. The Persians then besieged Jerusalem and took it by force. This account is not confirmed by other historians and the precise chronology of the Persian campaign in Syria is not clear. For a discussion of the surrender of Jerusalem see Butler, *op. cit.,* 59n.2.

7. It was walled up in the twelfth century and used only on Palm Sunday and on the Feast of the Exaltation of the Cross.

8. For a discussion of the claim that Heraclius systematically persecuted the Jews see J.B. Bury, *History of the Later Roman Empire*, New York, 1958, vol. 2, 215.

9. As Cyrus the Mukaukas did not become patriarch of Alexandria until 631 that letter was probably sent later.

10. In the Arabic language there was only one name for the empire, *al Roum.* The people were called *Roumi,* 'Romans.' Thus, in all the Arabic translations the Byzantines are referred to as 'the Romans'.

11. According to Sebeos.

12. Barhebreus, *Chronicon*, 274.

13. According to Sebeos.

14. It was at Hieria near Chalcedon that Heraclius was said to have developed his fear of wide open spaces. He was becoming severely ill and died in 641.

7. The First Inquisition

1. The monastery was probably situated on the route of the pilgrims from North Africa, north-west of Wadi el Natrun and south of Mariut. Its impressive ruins have been described by a medieval Arab traveller, who noted that the site had been long abandoned and used by the Arabs to lie in wait for travellers. The ruins can no longer be found and their exact position is not known.

2. It may have contained a portion of the 'True Cross'.

3. This in itself suggests that Cyrus had the support of Heraclius for his policy

of terror. Heraclius tried to root out sectarian division by an imperial edict, but when his policy failed he probably sanctioned the use of force as the last resort.

4. Severus. For the English translation see B. Evetts, *Severus of Al Ashmunein, History of the Coptic Church of Alexandria* (Paris 1915).

5. See E. Amélineau, *Monuments pour servir à l'histoire de l'Égypte Chrétienne aux IV-VII siècles* in *Mémoires de Mission Archéologique Française au Caire* (Paris 1888-95), vol. 2, 774ff.

6. Ansina or Antinoe was at this time the capital of the Thebaid. It lay opposite Hermopolis Magna, north of Lycopolis or Assyut.

7. According to Severus, *op. cit.*, it was either in or near Alexandria. Severus goes on to add that 'all the monks were pure-bred Egyptians, not a single foreigner among them'.

8. R.H. Charles, *The Chronicle of John, Coptic Bishop of Nikiu* (London 1916), 566.

8. Arabs at the Gates

1. The Arab historical accounts available to us were written centuries after the conquest. Many were based on a long oral tradition and reflected popular legends and apocryphal stories. Nevertheless, they are of unique interest, because they record events not mentioned by Byzantine historians and reveal how the Arabs perceived the Byzantines and their subjects, the Egyptian Copts.

2. Al Makin in *Historia Saracenica*, quoted in Butler, *op. cit.*, 206.

3. Al Nawawi and Ukhbah ibn A'amir quoted by Abu'l Mahasin; for translations see Butler, 202.

4. Butler, *op. cit.*, 206.

5. According to Eutychius and Makrizi; two months according to Yakut, as quoted in Butler, *op. cit.*, 211n.1.

6. According to Makrizi, the tribe of Rashida and some of the tribes of Lakhm joined 'Amr.

7. The hills mentioned by Severus, a phrase copied by Abu Salih, were probably those of Wadi Tumilat.

8. Makrizi said that at Umm Dunayn 'there was much fighting and victory delayed'; Abu'l Mahasin wrote: 'There was much fighting and it was now doubtful which side would have the victory'; quoted in Butler, *op. cit.*, 218.

9. See Al Mas'udi, *Collection d'Ouvrages Orientaux* (Paris 1863), 385-6.

9. The Fall of Babylon

1. Another general Theodore, to be distinguished from Heraclius' brother Theodore who lost the battles of Gabatha and Yarmouk.

2. Who relied on the account given by Ibn 'Abd el Hakam.

3. Some Arab writers mention that 'Amr used his *manganika* – 'mechanics' – against the fortress, but do not say if this proved of any use.

4. Some Arab sources cite the name of al Araj as the commander at Babylon, which is probably a corruption of 'George'. The disagreement between them on this subject is great and we have no clues as to who this 'George' might have been. Could it be a reference to St George, the patron saint of Babylon?

5. Those sources that cite the Copts as the defenders of the city can hardly be right.

6. Quoted in Butler, *op. cit.*, 256.

7. This account was given by Nicephorus.

8. 'God is the Greatest!'

10. Alexandria Won

1. The present village of Shabshir.

2. According to the *Chronicle* of John of Nikiu, Theodore had retreated in good order rather than being chased by the Arabs.

3. Possibly Malta or Gozo.

4. Whether he died of natural causes or at the hands of Martina is uncertain. Theophanes accused Pyrrhus in contriving the murder with Martina; Nicephorus and John claimed that Constantine's illness was of long duration. Sebeos wrote: 'Constantine died deceived by his mother.'

5. Was it the same one sent to him by Heraclius more than ten years previously?

6. Described by John of Nikiu; the relic of the Holy Cross was deposited in the convent of the monks of Tabennesi. It is not known what happened to it after the Arab conquest.

7. For the disagreement between them see below.

8. The order in which John of Nikiu gives these conditions is somewhat different.

9. The Arab tradition fixed that date, the first of Muharram, AH 21, as the date of the conquest. Some authorities think that this date applies to the second capture of Alexandria.

11. Mirror of Pharos

1. For Suyuti, see Appendix.

2. Quoted in Butler, *op. cit.*, 387.

3. Mistakenly known as Cleopatra's needles; they date to Tuthmosis III and were brought to Alexandria from Heliopolis by the Romans.

4. One of the obelisks was transported to London in 1871 and now embellishes the Thames Embankment. The other was taken to New York in 1880 and now stands in Central Park.

5. Descriptions by medieval travellers to Cairo suggest that the earliest minarets faithfully reproduced the three storeys of the Pharos.

6. Makrizi, *El Khitat*, vol. 1, 155.

7. He used the term 'zajaj mudabbar'.

8. Recorded by Ibn el Fakih, as quoted in Butler, *op. cit.*, 393.

9. Suyuti, *History of the Caliphs*, as quoted in Butler, *op. cit.*, 467.

10. Some reservations about the scale of the destruction still remain; see G. Botti in *Bulletin de la Société Archéologique d'Alexandrie*, no. 2 (1899), 15.

11. According to John of Nikiu, pp. 524, 548; E. Amélineau, *La géographie de l'Égypte à l'époque Copte* (Paris, 1893), 37-8 claimed that there was a second church by that name.

12. John of Nikiu, 543.

13. G. Botti, *L'Acropole d'Alexandrie*, 135, 137, 139, believed that the *Angelion* was originally a temple called the *Arcadion*. The *Angelion* survived the second Arab conquest and was reinstated by Patriarch Isaac at the end of the seventh century.

14. This number is confirmed by Ibn el Athir, Yakut and Ibn Khaldoun. Yakut adds that many people converted to Islam.

15. Yakut wrote 'three months'; Ibn Khaldoun mentioned one month, adding that 'the inhabitants were worn by the siege'.

13. Alexandria Lost

1. Quoted by Abu el Mahasin.

2. The word 'naqus' used here denoted more a wooden gong than a bell.

3. Ma'wardi, *Kitab el Akham el Sultaniya*, trans. Butler, *op. cit.*

4. For discussion of the disagreement of the Arab authors on the subject, see Butler, *op. cit.*, 451ff.

5. Found in *Vie du Patriarche Copte Isaac*, 5, 7, 73.

6. See W.E. Crum, *Coptic Ostraca: From the Collection of the Egypt Exploration Society, The Cairo Museum and Others* (London, 1902), no. 356.

7. Milne shows how the Muslims preserved the framework of the Byzantine system of government to this day in *Egypt under Roman Rule*, 216.

8. The German Islamic historian Gustav Weil (1808-1889), who quotes the letters in his work *Geschichte der Chalifen*, believed that his original source, Ibn el Hakam, had actually seen them; one of the earliest European authorities on the Arabic language, Baron Silvestre de Sacy (1758-1838) also confirmed their authenticity, basing his opinion on the archaic character of their language. I have followed the translations of Butler, *op. cit.*, 456ff.

9. This may indicate that the taxes raised by the Byzantines were higher; Abu Salih gives the figures variously as 20,000,000 and 18,000,000; see the discussion in Butler, *op. cit.*, 447-96.

10. This sentence was translated by Butler from Makirizi, *Khitat*, I, 78. Some of the letters were also quoted by Baladhuri, 219.

11. Fifty-two, according to Ibn Dukmak, see the discussion in Butler, *op. cit.*, 447-96.

12. The precise date is not certain.

13. According to el Tabari, as quoted in Butler, *op. cit.*, 469.

14. Afterwards Amr had him laid out in state at Fustat.

15. In the 680s it was rebuilt by the Coptic patriarch John III in a different location, and he was buried there; this building too was destroyed by Salah-ed-Din (Saladin) during the Crusader wars. The new cathedral of St Mark is a modern building off Sharia Horreya, opposite Sharia Nebi Daniel.

16. The road to Rhakotis cuts through the old Protestant cemetery where the British Consul Henry Salt, an amateur archaeologist who acquired many objects for the British Museum, was buried.

17. Many of the Arab historians did not distinguish between the two captures and the chronology of the conquest is often confused.

18. It is not entirely clear which church of St John Benjamin was referring to – there were two. The first stood south of the Pharos Lighthouse (Fort Khayt Bey) near Canopus, modern Abukir; it no longer exists. The second was the little shrine of St John the Baptist, built on the site of the ancient Serapeum; it was demolished during the crusades.

19. This sentence has been quoted time and again in modern literature about Alexandria; by, among others, E.M. Forster in *Alexandria: A History and a Guide*, and Lawrence Durrell in *The Alexandria Quartet*, where it is attributed to one of the characters.

20. See K. Gutzwiller, *A Guide to Hellenistic Literature* (Blackwell Publishing 2007), 47.

21. Archimedes' 'The Method' was fortuitously discovered in 1906 by Heiberg, lost and found again in 1998.

22. See L. Russo, *The Forgotten Revolution* (Heidelberg 2004), 8ff.

23. 'While I was in Fustat', wrote Masudi.

24. Quoted by Makrizi.

Epilogue

1. T. Vivian in G. Gabra, *Coptic Monasteries: Egypt's Monastic Art and Architecture* (Cairo and New York 2004), 17.

Bibliography

M. Awad, *Italy in Alexandria*, Alexandria: Alexandria Preservation Trust, 2009.

Baladhuri, *The Origins of the Islamic State*, trans. P.K. Hitti, New York: Columbia University Press, 1916

Barhebreus (Abu el Faraj), *Chronicon Ecclesiasticum*, ed. J.B. Abbeloos and T.J. Lamy, Louvain, 1872.

A.J. Butler, *The Arab Conquest of Egypt – And the Last Thirty Years of the Roman Dominion,* Oxford: Oxford University Press, 1902.

R.H. Charles, *The Chronicle of John, Coptic Bishop of Nikiu*, London: Williams and Norgate, 1916.

E. Doxiadis, *Mysterious Fayoum Portraits*, New York: Abrams, 1995.

H.A. Drake, *Constantine and the Bishops: The Politics of Intolerance*, Baltimore and London: Johns Hopkins University Press, 2000

L. Durrell, *The Alexandria Quartet*, London: Faber and Faber, 1962.

J-Y. Empereur, *Alexandria Rediscovered*, Paris: George Braziller, 1998.

J-Y. Empereur, *Alexandria: Past Present and Future*, London: Thames and Hudson, 2002.

P.M. Fraser, *Ptolemaic Alexandria*, Oxford: Oxford University Press, 1972.

E.M. Forster, *Alexandria: A History and a Guide*, New York: Anchor Books, 1961.

E.M. Forster, *Pharos and Pharillon: an Evocation of Alexandria*, London: Michael Haag Ltd, 1983.

C. Freeman, *The Closing of the Western Mind; the Rise of Faith and the Fall of Reason.* New York: Vintage Books, 2002.

G. Gabra, *Coptic Monasteries; Egypt's Monastic Art and Architecture*, Cairo and New York: American University in Cairo Press, 2002.

E. Gibbon, *The Decline and Fall of the Roman Empire*, ed. H.F. Mueller, New York: Modern Library, 2003.

K. Gutzwiller, *A Guide to Hellenistic Literature*, Oxford: Blackwell Publishing, 2007.

M. Haag, *Alexandria: City of Memory*, New Haven and London: Yale University Press, 2004.

J. Kamil, *Coptic Egypt; History and Guide*, Cairo and New York: American University in Cairo Press, 1990.

C.P. Kavafy, *Collected Poems*, trans. E. Keeley and P. Sherrard, London: Chatto & Windus, 1963 and 1968.

E. Keely, *Kavafi's Alexandria*, Princeton: Princeton University Press, 1996.

C. Kingsley, *Alexandria and Her Schools*, Edinburgh: McMillan, 1854.

R. MacLeod (ed.), *The Library of Alexandria: Centre of Learning in the Ancient World*, London: I.B. Tauris, 2001.

F. Mackler, *Historie d'Heraclius par l'évêque Sebeos*, Paris: Leroux, 1904; English translation by R. Bedrosian, *Sebeos, Bishop of the Bagratid Princedom*, New York: Sources of the Armenian Tradition, 1985.

N. Mahfouz, *Miramar*, Cairo: American University in Cairo Press, 1978.

Bibliography

Makrizi, *El Khitat ...*, Boulaq, 1854, trans. V. Bouriant as *Descriptions Topographiques et Historiques de l'Égypte*, Paris, 1895-1900.

Makrizi; Taqi el Din Ahmad ibn 'Ali, *Histoire d'Égypte de Makrizi*, trans. E. Blochet, *Revue de l'Orient latin* 8-11, 1900- 8.

Masudi, *Collection d'Ouvrages Orienteaux*, ed. Barbier de Maynard, Paris: Imprimerie Impériale, 1861-1917.

J. McKenzie, *The Architecture of Alexandria and Egypt 300 BC-AD 700*, New Haven: Yale University Press, 2007.

N. McLynn, *Ambrose of Milan: Church and Court in a Christian Capital*, Berkeley: University of California Press, 1994.

J. McManners (ed.), *The Oxford Illustrated History of Christianity*, Oxford: Oxford University Press, 1990.

J.G.A. Milne, *A History of Egypt Under Roman Rule*, Chicago: Ares, 1997.

J.J. Norwich, *Byzantium; The Early Centuries*, London: Penguin Books, 1990.

E. Pagels, *The Gnostic Gospels*, London: Weidenfeld and Nicolson, 1980.

E.A. Parsons, *The Alexandrian Library*, London: Cleaver Hume Press, 1952.

J. Pedersen, *The Arabic Book*, trans. G. French. New Jersey: Princeton University Press, 1984.

J. Pelikan, *The Christian Tradition; A History of the Development of Doctrine*, Chicago and London: University of Chicago Press, 1971.

J. Pollard and H. Reid, *The Rise and Fall of Alexandria*, London: Viking Press, 2006.

C.H. Roberts, *Manuscripts, Society and Belief in Early Christian Egypt*, Oxford: Oxford University Press, 1979.

L. Russo, *The Forgotten Revolution: How Science Was Born in 300 BC and Why it Had to be Reborn*, trans. S. Levy, New York, Berlin, Heidelberg: Springer-Verlag, 2004.

Severus of el Ashmunein, *History of the Patriarchs of the Coptic Church of Alexandria*, trans. B. Evetts, Paris: Firmin-Didot, 1915.

T. Vrettos, *Alexandria: City of the Western Mind*, New York: Free Press, 2001.

W. Wright, *Chronicle of Joshua the Stylite composed in Syriac AD 507*, Cambridge: Cambridge University Press, 1882.

Yakut, *Geographical Dictionary*, Leipzig: Wuestenfeld, 1866-73.

Index